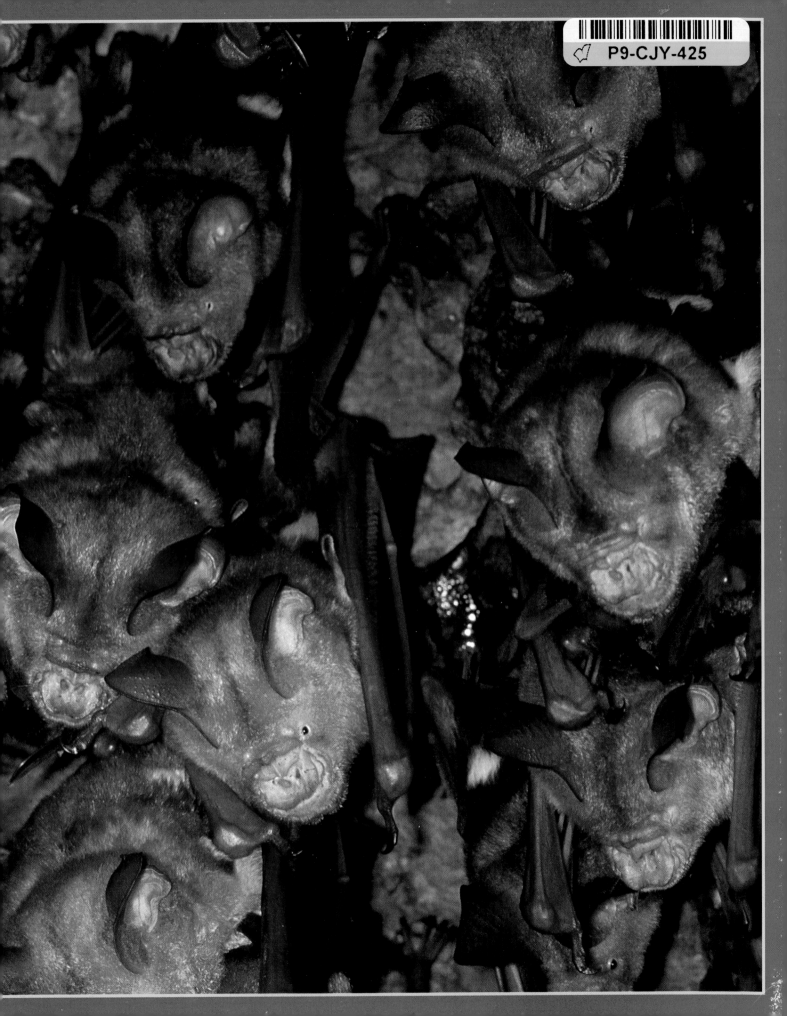

EYES ON NATURE™

CREEPY CREATURES

Incorporated

Copyright © 1998 Kidsbooks Inc.
3535 West Peterson Ave.
Chicago, IL 60659

Manufactured in the United States of America

Visit us at www.kidsbooks.com
Volume discounts available for group purchases.

Table of Contents

Scientific Consultant:
Barbara French
Conservation Information Specialist
Bat Conservation International

For even more information on bats, contact
Bat Conservation International (BCI) at
P.O. Box 162603, Austin, Texas, 78716-2603.
Their web site is http://www.batcon.org

BATS

GOING BATTY

Tonight, step outside into the darkness. Do you hear the flap, flap of unseen wings? Are small shapes flitting among the trees? You have caught a glimpse of the most fantastic night-fliers of the natural world—bats.

IS IT A BIRD?

Ancient people thought bats were featherless birds. We know now that bats, like humans, are mammals. They are warm-blooded and they nurse their babies. But, unlike humans, bats can fly!

▲ Other mammals that come close to flying, such as flying squirrels, use the winglike flaps of skin between their arms and legs to glide.

▲ The spotted bat has a black-and-white coat, pink wings, and enormous pink ears.

FUR FASHIONS

Mammals have fur, and bats are no exception. Those that roost outside have longer hair than those that roost in caves. Like cats, bats clean their fur using their tongue and claws. Although many bats are brown or gray, others are yellow, orange, white, or red. Some are so brightly colored, they're known as butterfly bats.

These Honduran white ▶ bats have snow-white fur.

DINOSAUR TIMES ▲

Fossil evidence shows that bats have been around for at least 50 million years. Some scientists think bats have been around even longer. Bats may have swooped around the huge heads of the dinosaurs 60 million years ago!

The smallest bat in North America, the pipistrelle, measures two and a half inches and fits neatly into a walnut shell!

ALL SIZED UP

The smallest bat is the smallest of all mammals—Thailand's bumblebee bat, which weighs less than a penny. The largest bats are the flying foxes of Asia, some of which have a wingspan of six feet—about the length of a surfboard! Their body is about one and a half feet long.

Vampire bats have razor-sharp teeth for slicing through skin!

DENTAL PLANS

A bat's teeth and the shape of its mouth are adapted to the type of food it eats. Fruit bats have large flat teeth for grinding pulpy fruit. Insect-eaters have jagged teeth in their cheeks that can slice and grind an insect's hard outsides.

BLIND AS A BAT

Many people think that bats are blind. In fact, some bats see well in dim light. Other bats see less well. But all bats have other, strong senses that help them find food in the dark, and help them navigate when flying.

▲ The long-nosed bat licks the fruit of an organ-pipe cactus.

9

BIG DIET

You may think of bats as blood-suckers. But in the real bat world, a bat diet may include fruit, leaves, pollen, cacti, insects, frogs, fish, spiders, lizards, and other bats! Bats are actually categorized into two groups—the large fruit-eating megabats, and the smaller microbats, most of which eat insects.

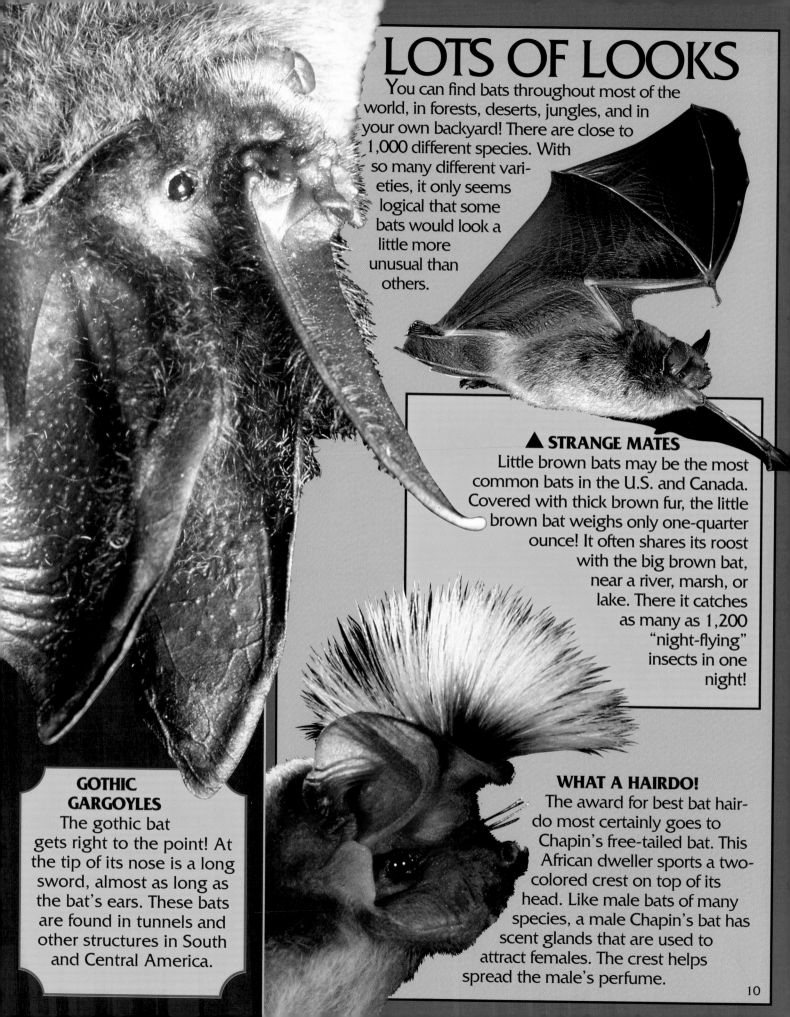

LOTS OF LOOKS

You can find bats throughout most of the world, in forests, deserts, jungles, and in your own backyard! There are close to 1,000 different species. With so many different varieties, it only seems logical that some bats would look a little more unusual than others.

▲ STRANGE MATES

Little brown bats may be the most common bats in the U.S. and Canada. Covered with thick brown fur, the little brown bat weighs only one-quarter ounce! It often shares its roost with the big brown bat, near a river, marsh, or lake. There it catches as many as 1,200 "night-flying" insects in one night!

GOTHIC GARGOYLES

The gothic bat gets right to the point! At the tip of its nose is a long sword, almost as long as the bat's ears. These bats are found in tunnels and other structures in South and Central America.

WHAT A HAIRDO!

The award for best bat hair-do most certainly goes to Chapin's free-tailed bat. This African dweller sports a two-colored crest on top of its head. Like male bats of many species, a male Chapin's bat has scent glands that are used to attract females. The crest helps spread the male's perfume.

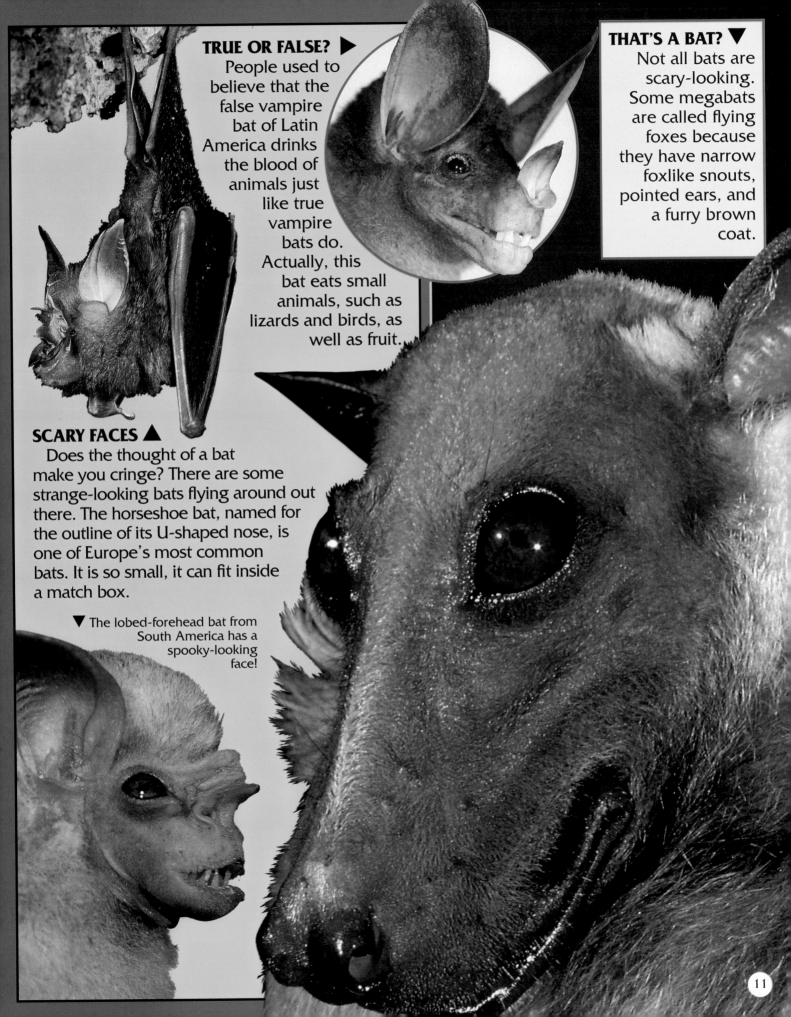

TRUE OR FALSE? ▶
People used to believe that the false vampire bat of Latin America drinks the blood of animals just like true vampire bats do. Actually, this bat eats small animals, such as lizards and birds, as well as fruit.

THAT'S A BAT? ▼
Not all bats are scary-looking. Some megabats are called flying foxes because they have narrow foxlike snouts, pointed ears, and a furry brown coat.

SCARY FACES ▲
Does the thought of a bat make you cringe? There are some strange-looking bats flying around out there. The horseshoe bat, named for the outline of its U-shaped nose, is one of Europe's most common bats. It is so small, it can fit inside a match box.

▼ The lobed-forehead bat from South America has a spooky-looking face!

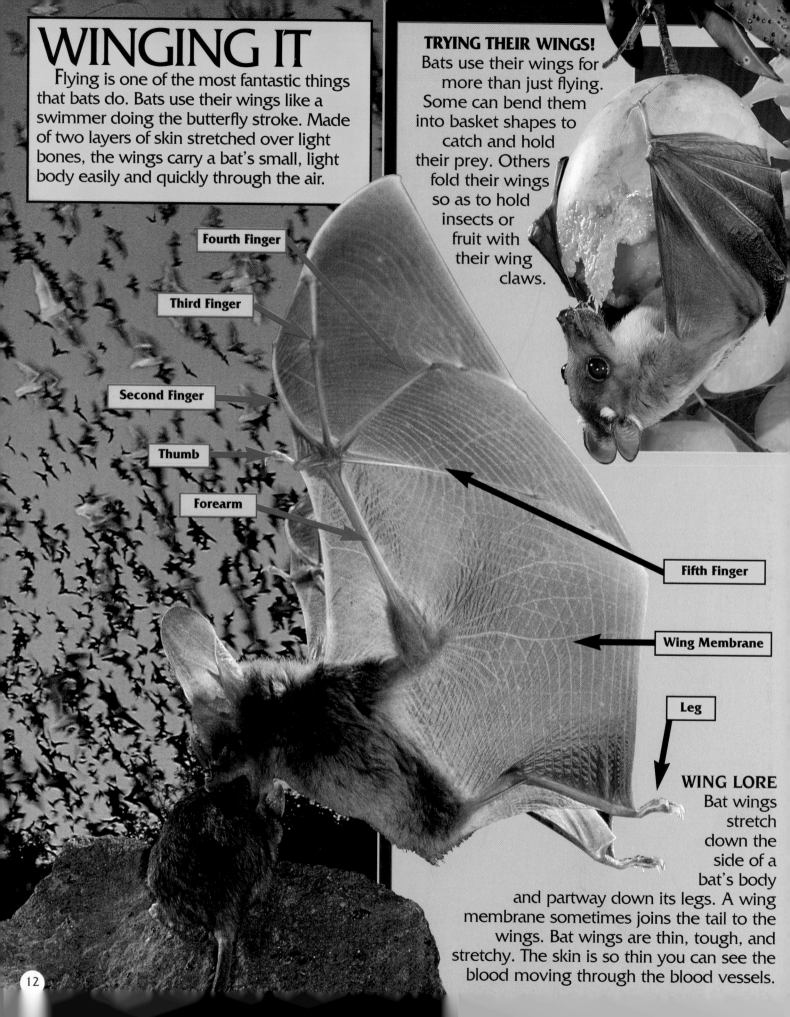

WINGING IT

Flying is one of the most fantastic things that bats do. Bats use their wings like a swimmer doing the butterfly stroke. Made of two layers of skin stretched over light bones, the wings carry a bat's small, light body easily and quickly through the air.

TRYING THEIR WINGS!
Bats use their wings for more than just flying. Some can bend them into basket shapes to catch and hold their prey. Others fold their wings so as to hold insects or fruit with their wing claws.

Fourth Finger

Third Finger

Second Finger

Thumb

Forearm

Fifth Finger

Wing Membrane

Leg

WING LORE
Bat wings stretch down the side of a bat's body and partway down its legs. A wing membrane sometimes joins the tail to the wings. Bat wings are thin, tough, and stretchy. The skin is so thin you can see the blood moving through the blood vessels.

KNEE ▶ ACTION

It's a good thing that bats can fly so well. They have legs, but are not very skillful at walking. A bat's knees bend backward, which makes these creatures very clumsy on the ground.

BIG GULP

Bats like to drink "on the wing." They fly over streams or ponds, slurping up water from midair. If they fly too low they go swimming, using their wings as paddles to push themselves through the water.

The long tail of a ▶ free-tailed bat may help it navigate.

WING SHAPES

Big brown bats have short broad wings for quick changes of direction. Mexican free-tails have longer narrower wings, perfect for long-distance flying. The Honduran white bat's short stubby wings let it hover in place like a helicopter.

HANGING OUT

On their wings, bats have a thumb and four long jointed fingers that are enormous compared to the size of their body. If you were a bat, your fingers would be longer than your legs! Bats also have hooked claws on their wings and toes which help them hang by their feet and climb along a wall or tree trunk. To leave their roosts, they simply fall towards the ground, flapping their wings until they take flight.

SUPER FLIERS

Mexican free-tailed bats are just one of 80 kinds of free-tailed microbats. They can fly 10,000 feet above the ground and, catching tailwinds, reach speeds of 60 mph— that's as fast as a car and as high-flying as an airplane!

13

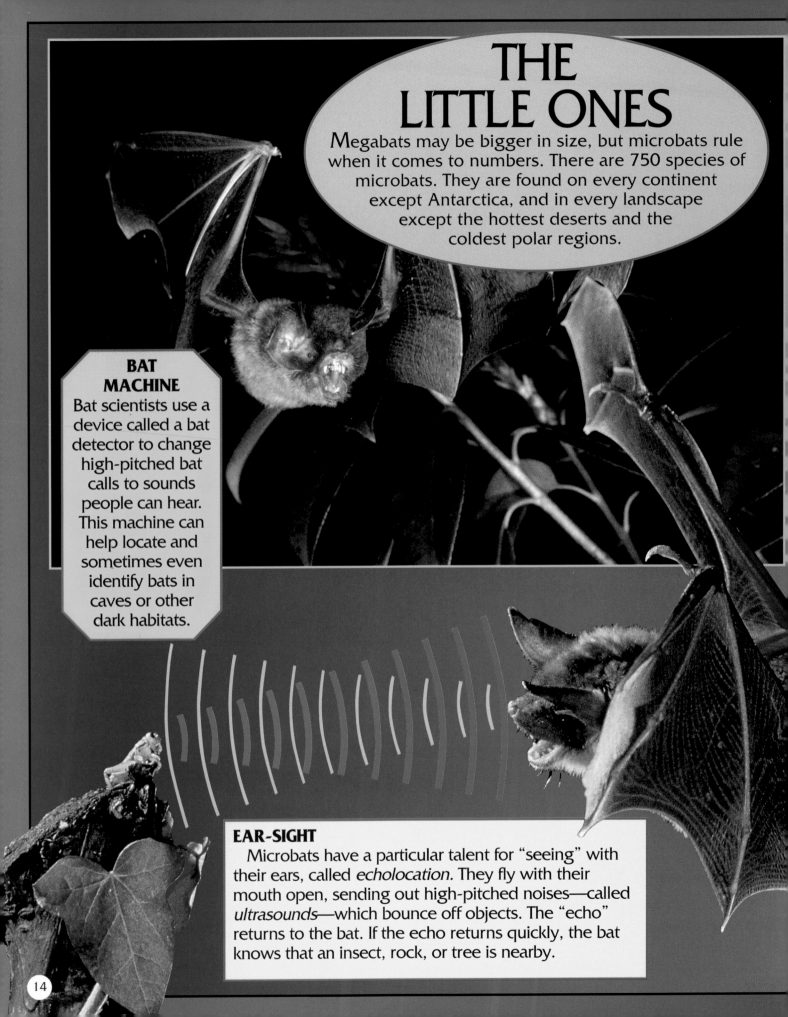

THE LITTLE ONES

Megabats may be bigger in size, but microbats rule when it comes to numbers. There are 750 species of microbats. They are found on every continent except Antarctica, and in every landscape except the hottest deserts and the coldest polar regions.

BAT MACHINE

Bat scientists use a device called a bat detector to change high-pitched bat calls to sounds people can hear. This machine can help locate and sometimes even identify bats in caves or other dark habitats.

EAR-SIGHT

Microbats have a particular talent for "seeing" with their ears, called *echolocation*. They fly with their mouth open, sending out high-pitched noises—called *ultrasounds*—which bounce off objects. The "echo" returns to the bat. If the echo returns quickly, the bat knows that an insect, rock, or tree is nearby.

Unlike many other microbats, the horse-shoe bat sends ultrasounds through its nose.

NOSE LEAVES

Some bats have folds of skin around their nostrils. These are called nose leaves. Scientists believe that nose leaves help with the process of echolocation by aiming a bat's sound waves in different directions.

Frog-eating bat ▶

LISTEN UP

Talk about good hearing! California leaf-nosed bats, which live in the lowland desert areas of the western U.S. and Mexico, can find bugs by listening for their footsteps or wing beats. They can even hear a cricket hopping!

FALSE
◀ **VAMPIRE**
The false vampire bat is the world's biggest microbat, measuring three feet from wing tip to wing tip.

▶ BIG EARS

The false vampire bat's huge ears are better to hear with. Big ears aid hearing by trapping more sounds. Many bats can tell the direction and speed of flying insects just by listening! This helps them find food in total darkness.

BIG BATS

Megabats "hang out" in warm areas, particularly near the equator. One hundred and fifty species live in Africa, India, Southeast Asia, the East Indies, and Australia. They eat fruit and flower nectar, which is plentiful year-round in tropical climates.

MEGA-SENSE

Unlike microbats, most mega-bats cannot echolocate. Notice how small their ears are! Megabats depend on other senses. Their large eyes, which can see very well, and their powerful sense of smell help them find ripe fruit at night.

▲ BABY ON BOARD

The Gambian epauletted bat is very "attached" to its offspring. This mother takes her pup with her when she goes searching for food. The baby hangs on to her belly fur with its strong claws as she flies, and shares the sweet fruit she finds.

◄ NECTAR NOSE

The nostrils of tube-nosed megabats open at the ends of short tubes. The bats stick these tube-like snouts deep into sweet-smelling flowers and suck up a tasty meal of nectar.

COOLING OFF
When flying foxes roost in the branches of large trees, they wrap their huge wings around their upside-down body to keep warm. On hot days, they cool off by fanning their wings.

MEGA CLAWS
Megabats have an extra feature which helps them to hold fruit with their wings— a claw on their second finger. These claws are an easy way for amateur bat-watchers to identify fruit bats.

SPECTACLES
The spectacled flying fox gets its name from the light rings around its eyes. Like other flying foxes, this bat lives where it is warm all year long. A powerful flier, it might travel as far as 20 miles to reach a favorite fruit orchard.

A DRINK OF BLOOD

No bat has been so feared and misunderstood as the vampire bat—the only bat that feeds on blood. Just forget those Count Dracula movies! Vampires rarely bite people or kill their prey. And an animal bitten by a vampire bat will not bleed to death, though it may contract a disease.

WHO'S WHO?

Vampire bats live in Mexico, Central America, and South America. The common vampire bat preys on cattle, horses, and other livestock. The hairy-legged vampire (above) targets birds. White-winged vampires feast on both mammals and birds.

WILD WALKER

All bats are great fliers, but the vampire bat is a great walker. The vampire can jump on all four legs like a frog, leap straight up into the air, or walk around on two legs like a monkey! This one is doing a handstand.

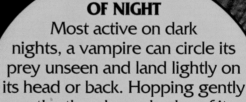

DEAD OF NIGHT

Most active on dark nights, a vampire can circle its prey unseen and land lightly on its head or back. Hopping gently on the thumbs and soles of its feet, it doesn't even waken the sleeping cow or chicken— even when it takes a bite!

NO SUCKER!

A common vampire doesn't suck blood. It laps it up. The bat has heat-sensitive pits on its face that help it pick a choice spot to bite. Then, using its razor-sharp teeth to cut a shallow wound in its prey, it presses its lower lip against the wound and starts licking!

JUST A DROP

The common vampire drinks about one ounce of blood a night. Blood is very thick. If a vampire drank too much, it would become too heavy to fly away!

By helping each other, vampire ▲ roost-mates help their species to survive.

HELPING OUT

Vampire bats are known to care for orphaned pups. They also feed other adults, which can be a life-saving act. If a vampire bat goes hungry for two days, it will die.

19

NIGHT HUNTERS

Meat-eating bats have good reasons for their nocturnal schedules. When they fly out at night to hunt for insects, fish, or small animals, most of their competition is sleeping.

A little big-eared bat ► holds its katydid prey.

TEETH TALE

When the oldest bat fossil was found in North America, scientists were amazed by how little bats have changed over the last 50 million years. The fossil's teeth showed that this prehistoric bat, like most of today's bats, was an insect-eater.

SCOOPING INSECTS

Most bats eat insects, catching their prey in their mouth or using their wings or tail membranes to scoop up insects. Small insects are eaten "on the wing." Larger ones may be eaten while the bat hangs from its roost by one foot and uses the other to hold its meal up to its mouth.

◄ FROG-EATERS

Some frog calls are inaudible to us, but not to the frog-eating bats of Mexico and southern Brazil. Not only can they follow a frog's call and catch a juicy morsel, but they can distinguish who's bite-sized and who's poisonous.

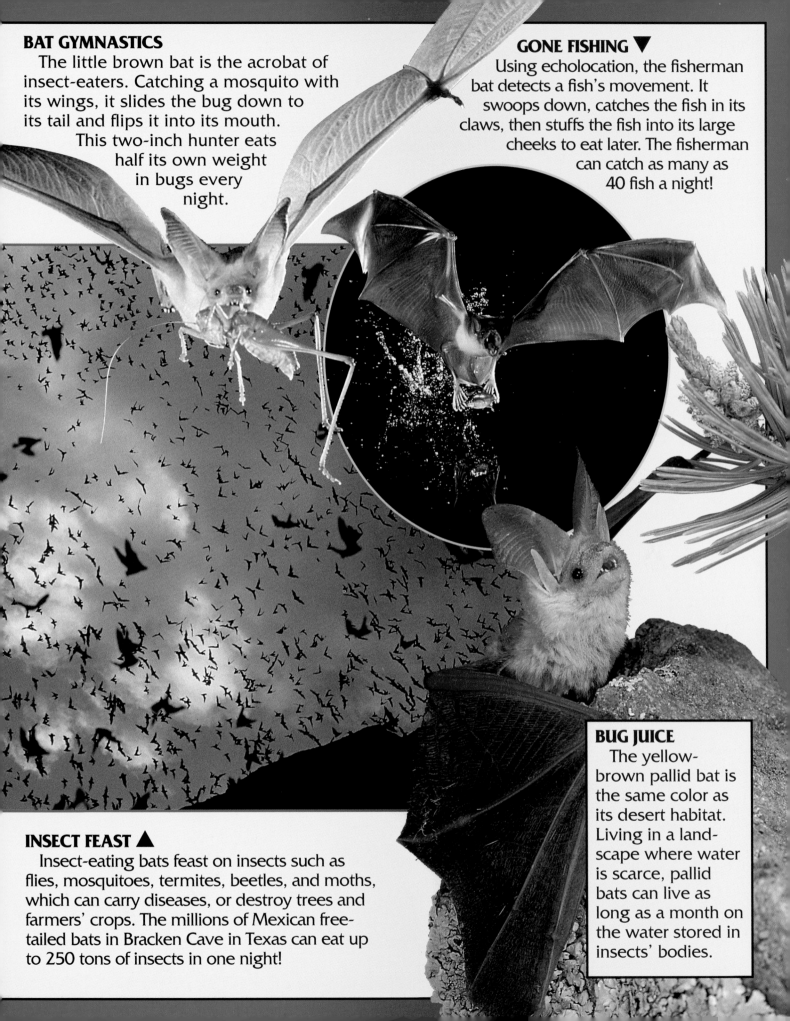

BAT GYMNASTICS

The little brown bat is the acrobat of insect-eaters. Catching a mosquito with its wings, it slides the bug down to its tail and flips it into its mouth. This two-inch hunter eats half its own weight in bugs every night.

GONE FISHING ▼

Using echolocation, the fisherman bat detects a fish's movement. It swoops down, catches the fish in its claws, then stuffs the fish into its large cheeks to eat later. The fisherman can catch as many as 40 fish a night!

BUG JUICE

The yellow-brown pallid bat is the same color as its desert habitat. Living in a landscape where water is scarce, pallid bats can live as long as a month on the water stored in insects' bodies.

INSECT FEAST ▲

Insect-eating bats feast on insects such as flies, mosquitoes, termites, beetles, and moths, which can carry diseases, or destroy trees and farmers' crops. The millions of Mexican free-tailed bats in Bracken Cave in Texas can eat up to 250 tons of insects in one night!

This Gambian fruit bat is feasting on figs.

FRUIT BATS

Although some bats eat a combination of fruit and insects, others eat fruit or nectar almost exclusively. Flying foxes chew and suck on fruit, swallowing the juice and spitting out the pulp.

▲Baobab tree

◀ LEAF TREATS

Although they get most of their nutrients from fruits, some fruit-eaters have to eat a certain amount of insects for protein. Fruit-eaters can also get protein from leaves. They soften the leaves in their mouth, swallow the liquid, and spit out the rest.

Bats help pollinate cacti and other flowering plants.

GIVING LIFE

Known as the "Tree of Life" because of its importance to other wildlife in Africa, the baobab (BAY-uh-bab) tree depends on bats to help it pollinate. Baobab flowers bloom at night, attracting nectar-eating bats. Pollen comes off on these bats' fur as they feed, and when they fly from blossom to blossom they carry the pollen with them!

Dipping its long tongue into a banana flower, this fruit bat finds a tasty meal.

◀ SMALL BUT FIERCE

The Queensland blossom bat has bristles on the tip of its tongue to help it lap up nectar. Don't be taken in by its delicate looks. It will attack any bat that elbows in on its territory!

BAT HEROES

Bananas, papayas, mangoes, avocados, and desert plants such as organ-pipe cacti rely on bats for pollination. Bats are responsible for scattering up to 95% of the seeds needed for new trees in the tropical rain forests.

23

TO THE BAT CAVE!

The place where a bat sleeps is called a *roost*. Some roosts are beds for only one or two bats. Other roosts are huge cities of thousands or even millions of bats. One popular roosting place is in caves.

WHERE TO GO?

Like most animals, bats have to adapt to colder temperatures and limited food during winter. Some migrate south to warmer climates where food is more plentiful. Others hibernate until spring. The European barbastelle does both, going south to hibernate in caves!

TURNING HEADS

Along the walls of a cave, a bat can grasp any little nook with its claws, and hang upside down. While roosting, it can turn its head right-side up and look around. A bat's neck is so flexible, it can even turn its head backwards!

STAYING COOL

During hibernation, bats live on fat they stored during the summer. Their breathing slows down and their heart rate may drop from 400 to 25 beats a minute. They may sleep for as long as five months without eating or drinking.

FISHERMAN'S FRIEND

The silver-haired bat roosts alone and migrates alone, flying thousands of miles to warmer climates. It has even been found on ships' masts out at sea, probably having been blown off course by a storm.

WHAT A CROWD!

Very sociable, Mexican free-tailed bats summer in U.S. caves. More than 20 million congregate in Texas's Bracken Cave, and 50,000 live in New Mexico's Carlsbad Caverns. When winter comes, they migrate south—1,500 miles to central Mexico.

WATER WEAR

As a bat hibernates, water from the cold air settles on its warm body. This condensation is a perfect refreshment when the bat wakes up thirsty!

EXCEPTIONAL ROOSTS

Caves are not the only roosting spots for bats. Bats hang out in trees, mines, tunnels, old buildings, bridges, bushes, abandoned termite nests, and tropical spider webs—anywhere they can sleep in safety and seclusion.

▼ An attic is a great place for bats to hang out.

The rafters in a barn are a welcome home to weary bats.

LEAF ARCHITECTS

Tiny tent-building bats roost in palm leaves in the jungles of Central and South America. To make a leaf "tent" to protect them from the rain, sun, and wind, these bats chew holes in the central rib of a big palm leaf until the leaf folds in half. The holes are then used as claw holds.

26

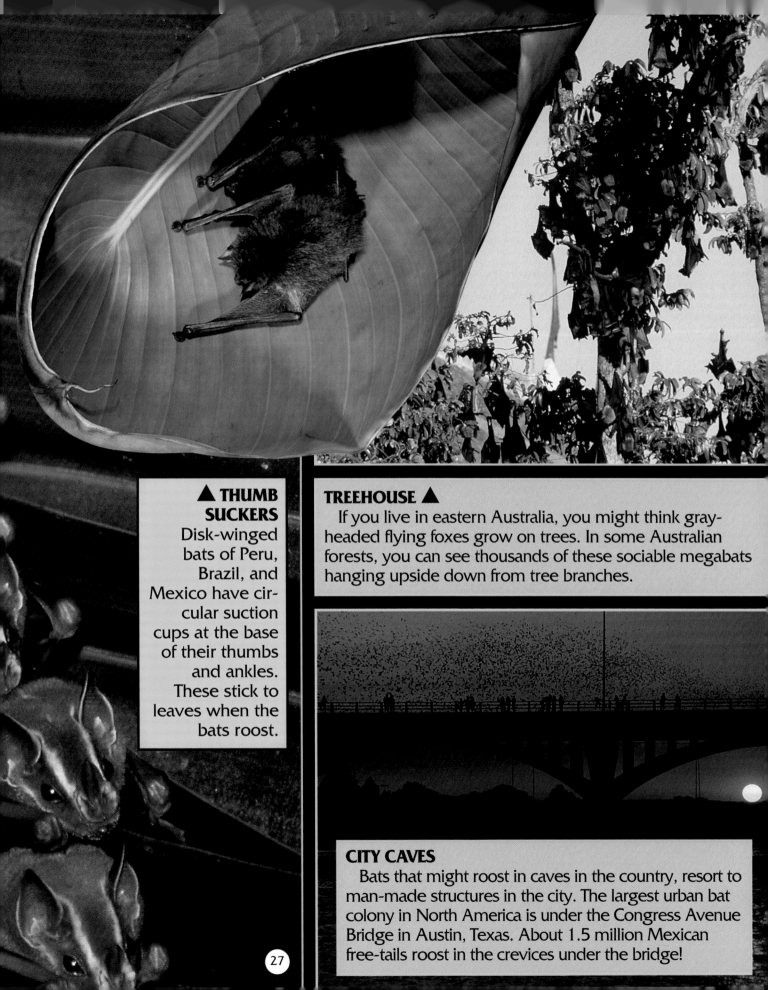

▲ THUMB SUCKERS
Disk-winged bats of Peru, Brazil, and Mexico have circular suction cups at the base of their thumbs and ankles. These stick to leaves when the bats roost.

TREEHOUSE ▲
If you live in eastern Australia, you might think gray-headed flying foxes grow on trees. In some Australian forests, you can see thousands of these sociable megabats hanging upside down from tree branches.

CITY CAVES
Bats that might roost in caves in the country, resort to man-made structures in the city. The largest urban bat colony in North America is under the Congress Avenue Bridge in Austin, Texas. About 1.5 million Mexican free-tails roost in the crevices under the bridge!

BEGINNING LIFE

In the spring, when there is plenty of food around, female bats waken from hibernation, or return from their southern migrations, and begin having pups. These bat babies may look small when they are born, but they grow up fast. Some are flying and hunting on their own when they are only one month old!

MULTIPLE PUPS

Cave dwelling bats usually give birth only once a year, but the big brown bat occasionally produces twins, triplets, and even quadruplets! Most of these multiple pups are born in June or July.

This red bat mother and her twins hang from their roost.

TINY TEETH

Pups are born hairless, and with a full set of teeth. These "milk" teeth are hook-shaped to grip their mother's nipples. Mothers nurse their babies for one to three months. When pups begin eating solids, they grow teeth better adapted for their diet.

BABY CATCH ▲

Some pups are born with the help of gravity. The mother bat hangs onto her roost with her wing claws, flips right-side up, gives birth, then catches the baby in her tail membrane. She has to move fast before the pup falls to the ground!

◄ HANGERS ON

Newborn pups are already experts at hanging around! As soon as they are born, they cling to their mother as she roosts, or to the roost itself. Because hanging on is so important, pups are born with strong feet and legs, and sharp claws. If a baby bat loses its grip and falls to the ground, it will most likely die.

SPECIAL VOICE

When a female bat returns to the nursery after hunting, how can she tell which of the many pups is hers? Easy! She recognizes its voice! And just to make sure she has found the right one, she smells and licks it. Only after it has passed these tests does she allow the hungry little bat to begin nursing.

ONE AND ONLY

Many small mammals have litters of seven or more babies once or twice a year. Almost all female bats give birth to only one baby once a year. This means that it can take a long time for bat colonies to recover if a roost is disturbed and bats are killed.

NURSERY CAVES

Some caves house millions of bats. In the Mexican free-tail nurseries in Bracken Cave, there can be as many as 500 babies per square foot! Bats often return to the same nursery site year after year. Scientists believe that the bat nursery at Carlsbad Caverns has been in use for 17,000 years!

These bats have been tagged and accounted for!

BAT ALERT

Over half of the bats in the U.S. and Canada are threatened or endangered. Scientists keep a close eye on endangered bats. They tag them, trace migrations, and monitor populations.

IN CAVES

If you visit a bat cave during the winter, don't disturb the bats! They can use an entire month's supply of fat trying to escape, and may starve before spring. Vandals at the Eagle Creek Cave in Arizona have reduced 30 million bats —once the world's largest colony— to 30,000!

UGLY RUMORS

Bats aren't dangerous to people. They do not get tangled in people's hair, and they do not "carry" rabies. Bats *can* "contract" rabies like any other wild animal can. For this reason, you should never handle them.

▼ It takes patient observation to study bats.

◄ Tagging a tiny bat requires a delicate and careful hand.

NATURAL FOES ▲

A number of animals prey on bats. Snakes climb to roosting places. Opossums, raccoons, and skunks prey on bats that fall to the ground. Owls and hawks catch bats as they emerge at dusk to hunt.

BAT HOUSE ▼
Because bats are losing a lot of their traditional roosting areas, people are building bat houses to make up for this loss. As many as 200 bats can fit in a house just two feet high. When mosquitoes began overwhelming the Florida Keys, a huge house was built to attract these masters of pest control.

◄ SPECIAL TREATMENT
Don't touch a hair on the head of Hawaii's only bat. Named for the silvery tips on their fur, hoary bats are so rare on the island, people can be jailed for disturbing them.

▶ IT'S THE LAW!
Because flying foxes eat fruit crops, many are being hunted and killed. People either don't know, or forget, that fruit bats actually help fruit to grow by spreading seeds around. Without bats to spread seeds and pollen, many tropical and subtropical forests around the world could not survive. Flying foxes are now protected by law in Australia's Ku-ring-gai preserve.

31

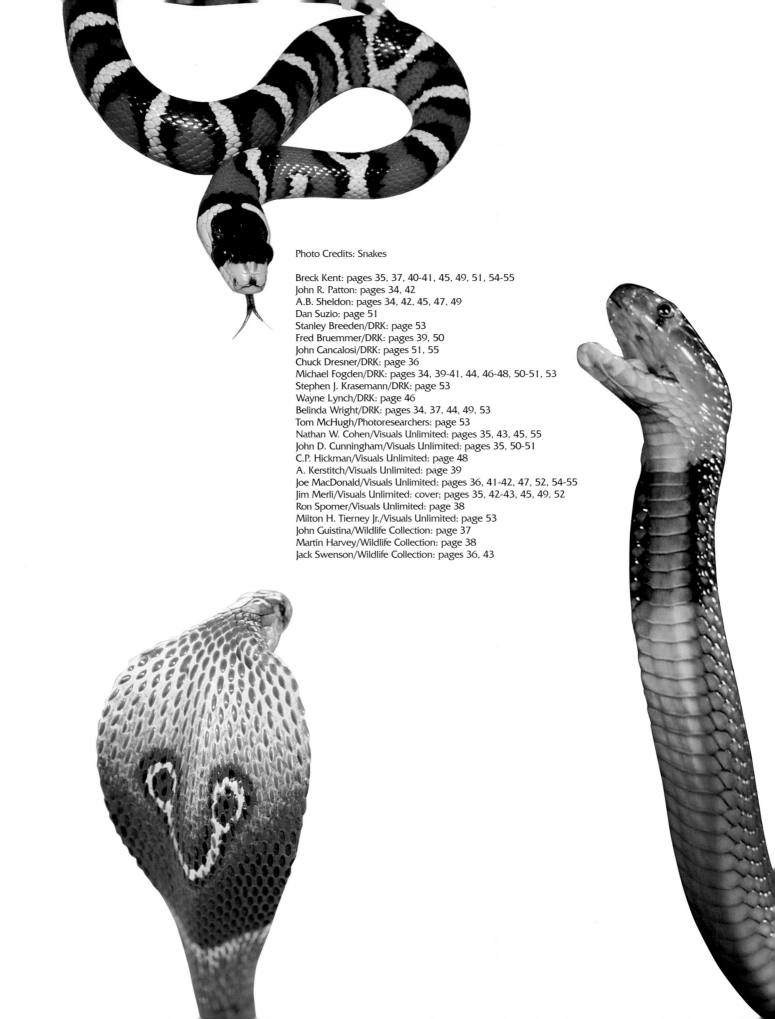

SNAKES

SO MANY SNAKES!

There are so many different kinds of snakes! In the 100 million years they've been on Earth, snakes have developed into 2,700 species. These slender reptiles come in many colors and sizes. A really big snake can grow to over 30 feet and weigh more than 300 pounds! And while the vast majority are harmless to humans, some snakes are deadly.

FABULOUS FANGS

When most people picture a snake, they see FANGS. But only poisonous snakes have fangs. Some serpents, such as rattlesnakes, have fangs that fold against the roof of the mouth, hidden but always ready to strike.

The fangs of the rough-scaled bush viper.

▶ At four and a half inches, the tiny thread snake is the smallest of all snakes.

▲ Pythons are the largest snakes.

▲ Basking in the sun helps keep a snake warm.

COLD LIKE A LIZARD

All snakes are reptiles. (Scientists who study snakes are called *herpetologists*, which comes from the Greek word *herpeton*, for reptile.) Like lizards—their closest relatives—snakes are cold-blooded. Their temperature depends on the air around them. If they are exposed to too much heat or cold, they will die. About 70°-90°F is ideal. Although found almost everywhere, no snakes can be found in icy polar regions.

▲ A kingsnake shedding its skin.

NEW SKIN

All their lives, snakes grow, but their skin doesn't grow with them. As the skin gets tight, the snake starts to shed. First, the skin coloring becomes dull. Even the scale covering the eye, called the *spectacle*, turns white. Then the snake rubs the skin off its nose and wiggles out.

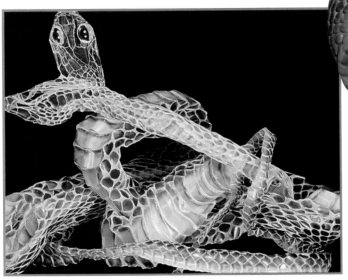

The scale pattern and spectacle are easy to see in shed skin.

SCALE TALE

Scales make the snake. They completely cover a snake and are part of the skin, which is smooth and satiny—not slimy. A special pattern of scales on the head identifies species. *Dorsal scales* cover a snake's back. On the belly are *ventral scales*, also called abdominal plates, which grip the ground as the snake moves.

SLENDER FELLA ▶

Snakes may not have legs but they have ribs—as many as 400. This long, flexible spine is the reason they can twist and turn and move on the ground and on trees. A snake has a body and a tail. All a snake's organs are narrow and line up end to end in its skinny body.

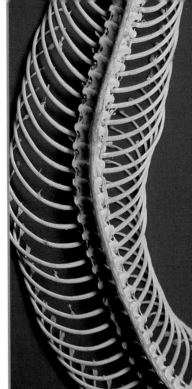

▼ This corn snake demonstrates how flexible its spine really is!

35

ALL IN THE FAMILIES

Besides the things they have in common, snakes have characteristics that set them apart. That's why there are eleven families of snakes. Those families with the most species, or kinds of snakes, are the boas and pythons, cobras and coral snakes, vipers, and typical snakes.

▼ The South American anaconda.

▲ One boa beauty is the emerald tree boa.

RAINBOW SKIN

Boas can be big, but they can also be small—and beautiful. Just look at the rainbow boa. This four-foot snake from Central America and northern South America has an unusual shining quality. Although only rusty brown with dark rings, the boa shimmers with color.

Rainbow boa

BIG BEASTS

In the boa and python family you'll find the largest snakes. What's big? In order to go eyeball to eyeball with the biggest ones, you'd have to climb three flights of stairs and look out a third story window! The anaconda (a boa) is nearly the longest (about 30 feet) and certainly the heftiest (over 330 pounds). It is found mostly near the water, preying on South American crocodiles called caimans.

◀ SWAYING SNAKES

The cobra family is a poisonous one, and contains many kinds of cobras, coral snakes, mambas, kraits, and sea snakes. Fast and graceful, the Indian cobras are famous for spreading their ribs and raising themselves off the ground.

The Australian death adder is often mistaken for a viper, but it's in the cobra family.

▼ Northern copperhead

VIPER SNIPER

Vipers, which include rattlesnakes and copperheads, are found all over the world, except in Australia.

PYTHON HEAVEN

Pythons are found in many places, but Australia and the nearby Pacific Islands are regions rich in these snakes. D'Albertis' Python (below) is found only in Papua New Guinea.

TYPICAL TYPES

The family of typical snakes dominates all regions of the world, except in Australia— where the cobra reigns. There are over 2,000 species in this group, out of the total 2,700 kinds of snakes! It's one big family, and it includes the harmless ratsnakes, corn snakes, kingsnakes, and garter snakes, as well as the poisonous boomslang, twig, and keelback snakes.

These corn snakes demonstrate how snakes can differ even within a species. One is *normal* (far left), another *melanistic* (has so much pigment that it's black), and the third is *albino* (lacking pigment in its skin).

WHERE THE SNAKES ARE

Snakes are specialists. They have behaviors suited to their *habitats*—the places where they live. And because they are cold-blooded, they adapt their behavior to the climate. Snakes in hot, dry regions seek cool, moist places underground. Snakes in cool areas hibernate in dens when it's cold.

▲ A western rattlesnake finds a neat nook in the rocks to keep cool.

▲ A sidewinding adder buries itself in the sand to escape the hot sun.

DESERT DWELLERS

Snakes are super desert survivors because their tough skin keeps them from drying out. Most desert dwellers need shelter from the heat and are only active at night, dawn, and dusk. Some, like the horned viper (right), have hornlike structures to keep sand out of their eyes and to protect them from the sun. Imagine! Serpent sunglasses!

It's spring, and these garter snakes are emerging from their den.

HAVING A BALL

Snakes that live in cooler climates hibernate when temperatures drop. Their heartbeats, breathing, and growth slow down so much that they are barely alive. They do this for just a few weeks or up to eight months—in a den. Snakes of different types hibernate together. They curl together to conserve heat, sometimes forming a "ball."

UNDERCOVER

"Burrowing" snakes live in burrows and are sometimes mistaken for worms. Short and cylinder shaped, they are toothless and eat worms and insects. They barely have eyes. The burrowing blind snake family has 200 members, none of which is more than 10 inches long. Not actually blind, they can see just well enough to get around in the dark underground.

Western blind snake

SURPRISING SWIMMER

They don't have flippers or fins, but snakes can swim. Snakes that live in the sea almost never leave the water. They have a paddlelike tail, which helps them swim, and they can stay underwater for a long time, possibly hours. Members of the cobra family, sea snakes have very potent venom.

The yellow-lipped sea krate.

TROPICAL PARADISE

A tropical forest is a snake's dream—with plenty of places to live. There's a floor for land rovers and rich earth for burrowing types. Also, there are trees, where a snake uses its tail like a monkey to hold on to limbs. Many snakes blend in with leaves or branches. Some, like the oriental whip snake (right), have a pointed snout so both eyes can look straight at an object—a fast-moving lizard or bird—and catch it.

▲ The fierce fer-de-lance is at home in the rotting tree stumps of the South American forest.

39

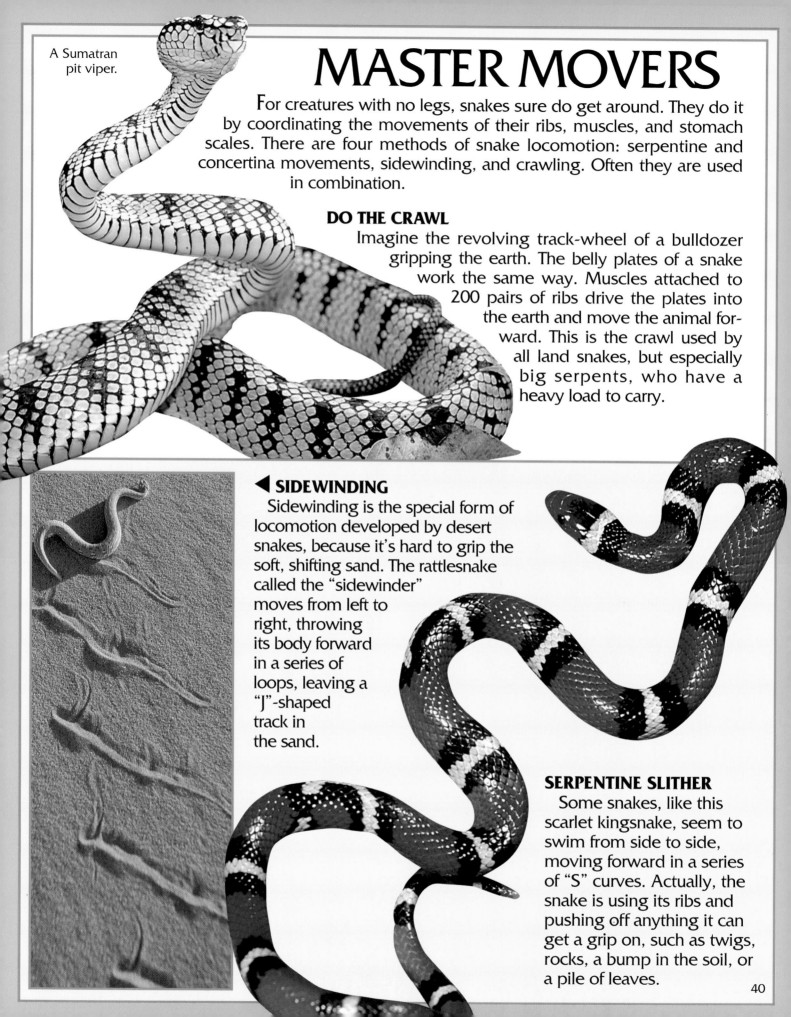

A Sumatran pit viper.

MASTER MOVERS

For creatures with no legs, snakes sure do get around. They do it by coordinating the movements of their ribs, muscles, and stomach scales. There are four methods of snake locomotion: serpentine and concertina movements, sidewinding, and crawling. Often they are used in combination.

DO THE CRAWL

Imagine the revolving track-wheel of a bulldozer gripping the earth. The belly plates of a snake work the same way. Muscles attached to 200 pairs of ribs drive the plates into the earth and move the animal forward. This is the crawl used by all land snakes, but especially big serpents, who have a heavy load to carry.

◄ SIDEWINDING

Sidewinding is the special form of locomotion developed by desert snakes, because it's hard to grip the soft, shifting sand. The rattlesnake called the "sidewinder" moves from left to right, throwing its body forward in a series of loops, leaving a "J"-shaped track in the sand.

SERPENTINE SLITHER

Some snakes, like this scarlet kingsnake, seem to swim from side to side, moving forward in a series of "S" curves. Actually, the snake is using its ribs and pushing off anything it can get a grip on, such as twigs, rocks, a bump in the soil, or a pile of leaves.

40

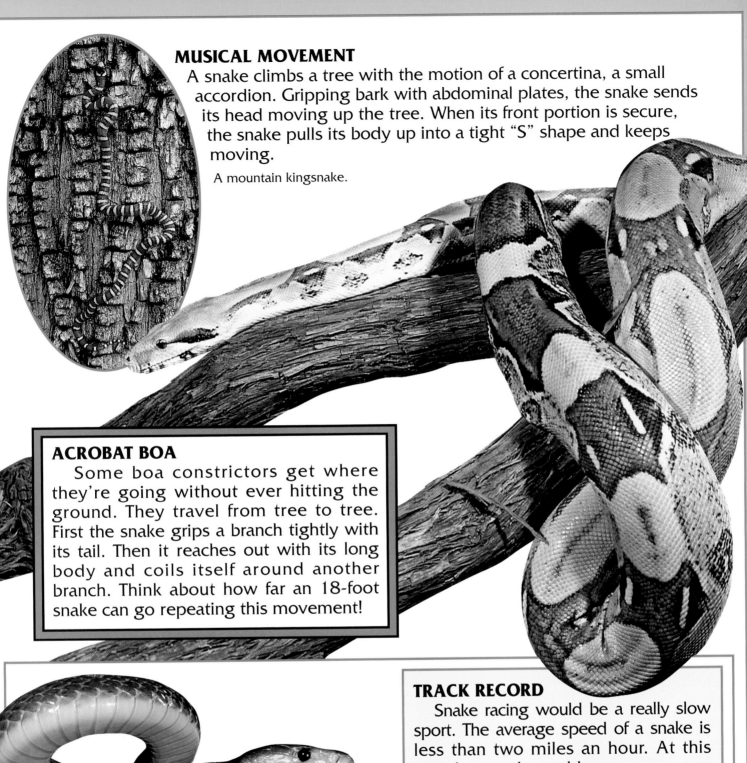

MUSICAL MOVEMENT

A snake climbs a tree with the motion of a concertina, a small accordion. Gripping bark with abdominal plates, the snake sends its head moving up the tree. When its front portion is secure, the snake pulls its body up into a tight "S" shape and keeps moving.

A mountain kingsnake.

ACROBAT BOA

Some boa constrictors get where they're going without ever hitting the ground. They travel from tree to tree. First the snake grips a branch tightly with its tail. Then it reaches out with its long body and coils itself around another branch. Think about how far an 18-foot snake can go repeating this movement!

TRACK RECORD

Snake racing would be a really slow sport. The average speed of a snake is less than two miles an hour. At this speed, no snake could overcome a running human (in short bursts, and on flat surfaces, the fastest runners reach speeds close to 27 miles per hour). But where there are rocks, bushes, and uneven footing, a snake could easily slither faster than a person chasing it.

◄ In eastern Africa, it is said that the black mamba can move at 10 to 12 mph and chases people aggressively.

41

SNAKE SENSE

Smell is a snake's most powerful sense, but not so much through the nostrils as through the forked, flickering tongue. The tongue picks up microscopic particles from the air and ground. Because it is forked, the tongue can pick up a scent from more than one direction at a time—left, right, down, up, straight ahead, and all directions in between. With this ability, the snake can zero in on its prey.

▲ A rattlesnake smelling an intruder.

◀ A kingsnake sniffing a trail.

▲ SNAKE SIGHT

Even if a snake's eyes are wide open, it doesn't see very well. Like this gaboon viper, most have eyes set on either side of their head, and they can't focus. But they can see when something moves. Prey animals have a better chance of escaping a snake if they stand still.

◀ EYE OPENER

No creature stares like a snake. Just look at this bush viper! Snakes have no eyelids, so they always appear to be staring, even when they're sleeping! The clear lens known as the spectacle, which is one of the snake's scales, protects the eyes. Under this shield, a snake's eyes moisten and move, and stare and stare.

▼ SNAKE EYES

The pupils of a snake's eyes are a telltale sign of its activities. Those snakes with round pupils travel during the day. These are called *diurnal* snakes. Snakes with pupils the shape of an oval slit from top to bottom are night, or *nocturnal*, hunters.

▲ The pointed shape of the vine snake's head helps it see straight ahead. These two daytime hunters seem to be working as a team!

This tree boa is a night hunter.

IT'S THE PITS

What do water moccasins and rattlesnakes have in common with pythons and boas? Pits! Facial pits are sensitive to heat. They help the snakes locate warm-blooded prey, especially at night. With pits between the eye and the nostril, a viper can "feel" a passing mouse and strike accurately, even in total darkness.

Note the pit of this eyelash viper!

GOOD VIBRATIONS

Snakes have no outer ears to spoil their smooth outline. But they do have an inner ear. They "hear" you coming by sensing vibrations on the ground through their jaw-bone, which sends the signals through connecting bones to the inner ear and brain.

43

A BIG APPETITE

Snakes eat meat, and that makes them *carnivores*. They kill three ways: They seize prey in their mouth. They squeeze with their coils. Or they poison prey using deadly fangs. Smaller species dine on insects, worms, lizards, and frogs. The largest species can swallow mammals the size of a small deer.

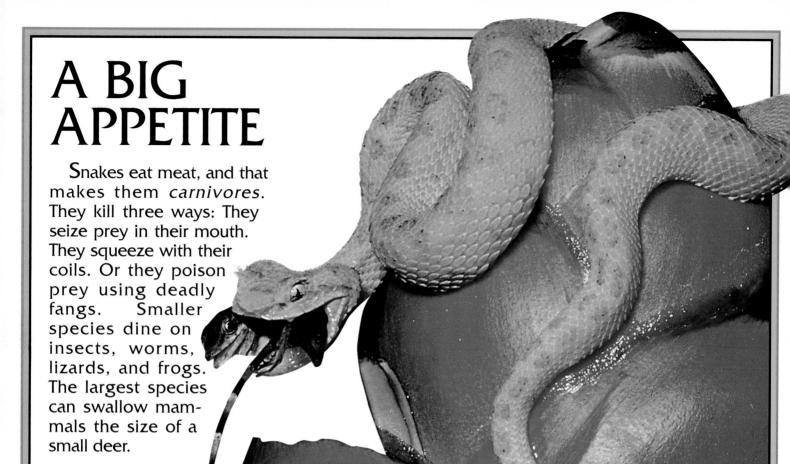

▲ An eyelash viper eating a lizard.

DON'T FORGET TO BREATHE!

When a snake eats, its mouth is completely filled. Even its air passage is blocked. How does it breathe? Its breathing tube slides forward to create an opening (left). Also, the tongue slides back into a little pocket . Meanwhile, saliva pours into the mouth to make the prey slide through the jaws easily. And backward pointing teeth dig in to keep even slippery frogs from escaping.

▼ Like the kingsnakes, this king cobra is named "king" because it makes a meal out of other snakes. It's also the longest venomous snake in the world.

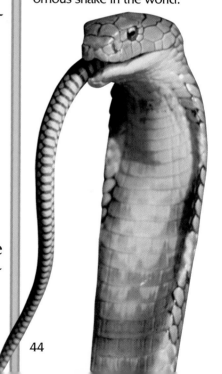

JAWS!

What can you fit in your mouth? Not much compared to a snake. A snake cannot chew or bite off pieces. It swallows its food whole—and usually headfirst. The secret is in the jaws. The lower jaw unhinges so the mouth opens WIDE. Also, the lower jaw has two separate halves connected by elastic tissue. The snake works one side and then the other, until the victim is swallowed.

STRIKE. YOU'RE OUT!

Vipers are the master predators of the snake world. When they strike, the fangs unfold, shoot directly forward, and stab the victim, filling it with poison. The snake then pulls back to avoid being injured. The poisoned victim usually runs away, but the venom slows it to a full stop, and the snake tracks it down.

THE BIG SQUEEZE

Pythons, boas, and their relatives really know how to squeeze the life out of prey. These *constrictors* grasp prey in their mouth and coil around it. They constrict, or squeeze, the prey until it can no longer breathe and the heart stops.

HARDLY HUNTERS

Most snakes don't hunt. They usually wait for prey to come to them. But some do go looking for food. There are also snakes that "fish." Like the copperhead above, they use their tail as "bait," luring prey into close striking range.

IN DIGESTION

A snake is so slim you can watch a meal travel to its stomach, pushed by strong muscles moving in waves. Digestion takes several days or even weeks, depending on the feast. Powerful stomach juices dissolve everything but hair and feathers. If the next meal is hard to find or the snake is hibernating, the snake can go for months without eating.

45

DEFENSE !

Snakes have enemies. Mongooses, roadrunners, secretary birds, and serpent eagles specialize in eating snakes. Raccoons, owls, coyotes, and others find them a good meal, too. Hiding is a snake's first line of defense. Scaring or intimidating an enemy works for some. Distracting is another measure. The ultimate maneuver is biting.

BACK OFF!

The rattlesnake uses several defense methods to tell an intruder to get out of its way. The snake may hold its forked tongue out stiffly. It may raise its body in the air. And it may rattle its tail. The noise of the shell-like rings on its tail is an alarming sound and would probably be enough to stop you in your tracks. It is said that the rattle can be heard from over 160 feet away!

A prairie rattlesnake about to strike! ▶

This twig snake puffs up to frighten enemies.

PUFFED UP

To a snake trying to scare away an intruder, being bigger seems better. The puff adder gets its name from puffing itself up to face an attacker. The snake expands its ribs so it looks larger and scarier than it is. The cobra is known for opening its hood. For added effect, the spectacled cobra has a scary mask on its hood.

HISSSSS! ▶

Snakes are silent because they have no vocal cords. But some do hiss to warn invaders. The bull snake is one of the loudest. A very thin membrane in the front of its throat makes the sound possible. The snake opens wide and blows hard against this membrane. The vibration causes the nerve-shattering hiss.

A spectacled cobra.

▼ SURPRISE!

Surprise is a good defense method and there are snakes who like to startle their enemies. The water moccasin has the nickname "cotton-mouth" because it opens a gaping white mouth to frighten intruders.

▼Opening the mouth is one defense tactic many snakes use.

SPITTING COBRA ▶

The African black-necked cobra spits poison to defend itself, and it can hit its mark from eight feet away! The snake raises its head, takes aim, and sprays venom through pinholes in the front of its fangs. Contact with the poison can cause eye damage or even blindness.

A bandy bandy from Australia, raising its body as a warning! ▼

SNEAKY SNAKES

Snakes have some pretty sneaky ways of fooling their enemies. Some have a built-in way of hiding called *camouflage*. Their skin color or pattern blends in with their surroundings. Some other tricky tactics include *mimicry* and *death-feigning*. Mimicry is when a non-poisonous snake has taken on the look of a poisonous snake.

NOW YOU SEE IT...
NOW YOU DON'T!

Snakes use all kinds of ways to disguise themselves. The green vine snake (above) hangs motionless in trees and looks like just another vine. The puff adder has a skin pattern that breaks the outline of its body so that it disappears among its surroundings. The twig snake has a head shaped like part of a tree.

Puff adder

Twig snake

HEADS OR TAILS ▼

The sand boa has a blunt tail that looks amazingly like its head. When threatened, this snake ducks its head, coils tightly, and sticks up its tail. Enemies mistakenly attack the tail. The sand boa knows a scarred tail is better than a squashed skull.

▲ The poisonous coral snake.

COLOR SHOCK ▲

Ringneck snakes blend in with their surroundings when they're on their stomach. If trouble comes near, they hold up their colored tail for shock effect. If that doesn't scare the trespasser, the snakes roll over on their back and really blast their enemy with color.

COLORFUL CORAL

The poisonous coral snake is small (about 3 feet), shy, and pretty. It's ringed with red, yellow, and black. So are a lot of harmless snakes. They are mimicking the dangerous coral snake so that predators will think twice about striking them. If you ever see a red-yellow-and-black snake, remember: Red touch yellow, kill a fellow. Red touch black, poison lack.

The harmless kingsnake. ▲

PLAYING POSSUM

If a predator should come around, the hognose flattens out its head and hopes to look scary. If this fails, the hognose "dies" right before the predator's eyes. It twitches and twists as if it is in pain and breathing its last breath. Then the snake flops over on its back, opens its mouth, and lets its tongue hang out. It may even peek to see if the enemy is gone before flopping back on its belly and crawling off.

SNAKES ALIVE!

▲ An eyelash viper mother and her newborns.

Imagine giving birth to 50 babies at one time. Boa constrictors do. They and many other snakes give birth to live offspring. Other snakes lay eggs. Some, like the reticulated python, lay 100 or more. After laying eggs or giving birth, most mothers, but not all, take off.

SHE'S MINE!

Reproduction begins with a snake's sense of smell. A scent trail leads males to females. Sometimes it may lead to a wrestling match if another male is around. With rattlesnakes, like the ones to the left, there is a "combat dance." The male snakes raise their body high into the air and push against one another. But they never bite. One finally falls over and slinks away. The other finds his mate.

▲ Garter snakes breed in big groups.

MATING GAME

When mating, a male and female entwine their two bodies and stay together for a few minutes or several hours.

HOT SPOT

A female laying eggs takes great care in finding a nesting spot that will provide shelter, moisture, and warmth for her eggs. In burrowed holes, beneath stones, and among rotting leaves are fine places.

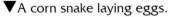
▼A corn snake laying eggs.

MOTHER WARMTH

The Indian python is one of the few snakes that "sits" on her eggs. After pushing the 50 to 100 eggs into a pile, she coils around them, resting her head on top. Then she contracts her muscles to raise her body heat and warms them.

TOUGH STUFF

Snake eggs are tough, not brittle like birds' eggs. They are leathery, soft, and flexible. The eggs start out oval and grow, changing shape as the snake inside develops. The snakes hatch by poking their way out with an "egg tooth," a kind of horn on their snout that breaks off after this one use.

▼A hog-nosed viper giving birth.

◀ LOOK ALIKE

Most baby snakes are miniature copies of their parents. Take a look at this boa constrictor and her newborn. Baby snakes may be colored and patterned differently. But some change as they develop and end up looking exactly like their parents.

SMART SNAKES ▶

Because there are no adults to care for them, young snakes must catch and kill their own food. At birth, they must be totally equipped to survive. Venomous snakes have sacs full of poison and fangs ready to use. As you can see from this newly hatched pine snake, babies are fully aware they must protect themselves.

DARING TO BE DIFFERENT

A two-headed snake.

▲This pink kingsnake is an albino.

Some snakes really stand out from the crowd. These distinct creatures may be different from other snakes in the way they behave—how they move, reproduce, or eat. They may live where most other snakes could not. Or, they may just look incredibly unusual.

REPTILE RHINO ▶

Hornlike formations do not seem very snakelike, but the rhinoceros viper of Africa has them. This serpent has a blue-and-yellow butterfly design. Its nickname is the "river jack" because the rhinoceros viper is found near streams and rivers.

EGGS ON THE MENU ▼

The African egg-eater chooses eggs for every meal. Big eggs. Opening its mouth incredibly wide, this serpent can swallow an egg twice as thick as its own body. As the egg moves down its throat, the snake pierces it with a sharp spine. The contents travel to its stomach, but the snake spits out the shell.

SOLE MATE ▲

Usually, it takes two to make babies, but there is one snake that does it all alone. The female Brahminy blind snake will not wait around if she can't find a mate. Her eggs will develop on their own, and her babies will all be female.

SNAKE OR FAKE? ▶

Is it just a weird snake or what? If so, where's its tail? Actually, this creature is a caterpillar from the rainforest in Costa Rica. By mimicking a snake, it hopes to frighten away predators.

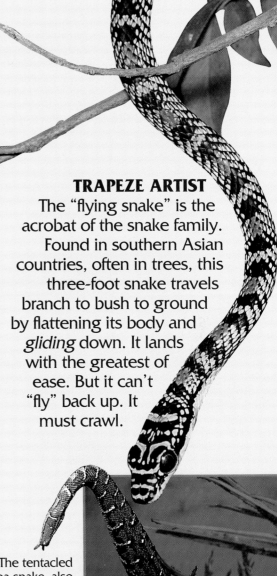

TRAPEZE ARTIST

The "flying snake" is the acrobat of the snake family. Found in southern Asian countries, often in trees, this three-foot snake travels branch to bush to ground by flattening its body and *gliding* down. It lands with the greatest of ease. But it can't "fly" back up. It must crawl.

The tentacled sea snake, also known as the fishing snake, lives in Southeast Asia.

The elephant's trunk snake is totally aquatic.

UNDERWATER SURPRISE

There are plenty of snakes that live in the sea, in lakes, or in rivers. Most of them look like snakes. But some look so unusual, they might fool you into thinking they're not snakes at all!

SNAKES AND US

Snake charmers fascinate their audience and the snake! The snake isn't charmed by the music, though. It is watching the swaying movement of the piper.

Today, when you say "serpent," many people think of the biblical story of the garden of Eden. But snakes have represented many other things besides evil, such as wisdom, death, and love. The Greeks saw snakes as a symbol of immortality—not that snakes live forever, but they do shed their skin to become new again.

Southern Pacific rattlesnake

ROYAL SNAKE EATER▼

When people find kingsnakes in their yard, they leave them alone because these serpents kill other snakes—even deadly rattlesnakes. A constrictor, the king grabs the rattlesnake behind the head and coils around the prey's body. The king is immune to the rattlesnake's venom, so very often it goes unharmed.

RATTLESNAKE ROUNDUP

Snakes are not the only ones that wear their skin. People make shoes, bags, and clothes out of snake skin. People also kill snakes for sport. What used to be a rattlesnake hunt in colonial times is now a roundup in which thousands of snakes are killed in a single weekend. As many as a half-million may be killed each year, most of them western diamondbacks.

DON'T TREAD ON ME

In the United States, where there are 15 species, rattlesnakes really get people's attention. The majestic 8-foot eastern diamondback is the largest. During the Revolutionary War, colonists chose this viper as a symbol because it doesn't attack unless threatened, it warns its victims, and it's fearless when struck. Flags flew with the snake's image and the words "Don't Tread on Me."

54

FARMER'S HELPER

A rat snake is a welcome sight to farmers. These snakes eat the rats and mice that destroy crops in grain stores. The corn snake may be the prettiest, but the yellow rat snake actually seems to enjoy people. As a pet, it's often found in the house curled up in a pot or drawer.

The endangered indigo snake.

SNAKE MEDICINE

The venom that poisons people is also used to make medicine. "Milking" snakes for their venom is done by holding their head and pressing, which causes the venom glands to squirt. The venom is used to make antidotes that erase the effects of the poison. The venom of vipers is also being used in medicines to treat high blood pressure, heart failure, and kidney failure.

PLAY MATE

Keeping a snake for a pet can be fun—and very interesting. Harmless North American snakes are best. Snakes like boas grow too big—in three years a baby boa could be five-feet long. A good snake house is an old aquarium or glass-fronted box with a mesh top. Snakes also need water, food, and kindness—like any other animal.

Although gentle, this gigantic Burmese python might not make the best pet. Where would you put it? And what would you feed it?

DISAPPEARING SNAKES

Some snakes are disappearing from the Earth because their habitats are becoming places for roads and houses. In the United States several snakes are endangered: the indigo snake of the Southeast, the ridge-nosed rattlesnake of southern Arizona, the Atlantic salt marsh snake of the eastern Florida coast, and the beautiful San Francisco garter snake.

San Francisco garter snake

SPIDERS

SPIDERS!

Down in the basement or up in the attic, out in the desert or high in the mountains—spiders are everywhere. And they've been here on Earth for more than 380 million years. There are about 30,000 known species, and maybe as many as three times more yet to be discovered. They can be as big as 10 inches across or smaller than the head of a pin. And a few have a pretty poisonous bite, more potent than a rattlesnake's!

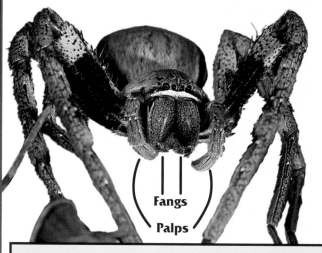

Fangs

Palps

DEADLY DENTURES
A spider's mouth is double trouble for prey. On each of its two jaws, a sharp, curved fang carries poison. Then, on each side of the mouth are leglike things called *pedipalps,* or *palps,* which are used to hold prey.

HUNTERS AND TRAPPERS
All spiders are *carnivores,* or meat-eaters, that dine mostly on insects. Those known as wandering spiders are hunters that search for prey. The web builders, however, spin sticky traps of silk and lie in wait.

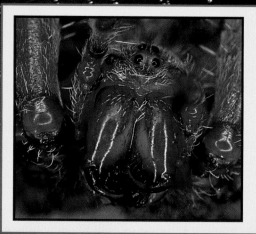

TRUE OR TARANTULA
Most common spiders are called "true spiders." Their jaws move from side to side (left). But the big, hairy spiders (right), most often called tarantulas in the United States, have large fangs and move their jaws up and down.

BACKBONES

What do you call an animal with legs and joints but no backbones? Scientists call them *arthropods* (ARE-thruh-pods). Like crabs, instead of having a skeleton on the inside, spiders have an *exoskeleton* on the outside, a tough suit of armor called a *carapace*, which protects the soft body parts.

◄ BREAK OUT

When a spider grows, its exoskeleton does not. So the spider molts. It replaces the small carapace with a bigger one. Depending on its size, a spider may molt from 3 to 12 times during its life. How does it do it? The spider hangs upside down by a silk thread until the exoskeleton splits, then simply pulls itself out, wearing a new carapace underneath.

SPIDERS VS. INSECTS

Spiders are not insects. Classified as *arachnids* (uh-RACK-nids), spiders have eight legs and two main parts to their body, and they can make silk. The arthropods known as *insects* are in the class *Insecta*. They have six legs, three main parts to their body, wings, and antennae.

▲ TWO-PARTS SPIDER

A spider's body is divided into two parts. The upper section is made up of the head, stomach, and poison glands. The lower section contains the heart, lungs, and other organs, as well as the silk glands.

FAMILY TIES

Every family has relatives. Spiders have scorpions and mites. These cousins have eight legs but different body types.

A mite, magnified.

A scorpion raising its tail.

SENSITIVE BODY

A long-legged wandering spider.

A leg with claw-like feet and sensitive hairs, magnified.

Spiders lack ears, so they do not hear as humans do. But they have legs that do a lot of "ear-work." Mostly on the legs, but also on the body, are hundreds of tiny slits that sense vibrations. With this leg sense, spiders know when an insect walks by or lands on a web.

▲ HAIRY SENSATIONS

Spiders feel objects they touch directly, and they also "feel" vibrations in the air, ground, and water. Sensory hairs are spread all over the spider's body. Each connects to nerves, which connect to the brain. Touch one hair, and the jumping spider (above) will know you're there.

SHED A LEG

If a leg is lost or damaged, spiders grow new ones. Sometimes spiders will shed a leg on purpose to escape a predator. The *regeneration*, or regrowth, of legs takes place as long as a spider is still molting.

▲ TASTE BY TOUCH

Putting their best foot forward, spiders taste with their feet. Hollow hairs on the end of their legs and palps take in chemicals from food, and this pro-duces taste. So when spiders hold or touch food, like this crab spider holding a bumblebee, they are probably tasting it.

EYESIGHT

Most spiders have eight eyes! Some have six or four or fewer. All these eyes sit on the spider's face. Web builders have poor vision. But some hunting spiders can see well in several directions at once, like the amazing wolf spider (left), a creature that can spot objects a foot away!

HANGING ON ▼

A spider's legs are tools for balancing. Each one is flexible, with seven sections connected by joints. Wandering spiders have two claws and a tuft of hair on each foot to help them cling to slippery surfaces. Web builders, like this black widow, have three claws on each leg. The one in the middle grips fine silk strands.

▲ Fangs and palps

▶ This grasshopper will soon be soup.

LIQUID DIET

Liquids are all that spiders can eat, so they have to turn their prey to juice. Through their fangs, spiders inject victims with poison, then with digestive fluids. The prey's soft insides become like soup, and spiders can then suck up their meal.

61

SILKY WORLD

Silk emerges from an orb weaver's spinnerets.

A spider without silk is like a fish without water. Silk is the material of webs, traps, egg sacks, and burrow linings. It is produced by glands, as many as seven, deep inside a spider's body. It can be dry or sticky, fuzzy or smooth, thick or thin.

SILK SOURCE

Silk is still liquid as it leaves the spider's body. It emerges through *spinnerets*, which are flexible, fingerlike tubes, near the end of the body. As the spinnerets pull and bend the silk, the material hardens.

LIFELINE

Whenever they travel, spiders form a *dragline*, a double thread that trails behind them. With it, they can return home quickly and easily. If danger should approach, spiders use the dragline to escape, dropping out of sight and hanging on until the threat passes.

A black-and-yellow garden spider casting its dragline.

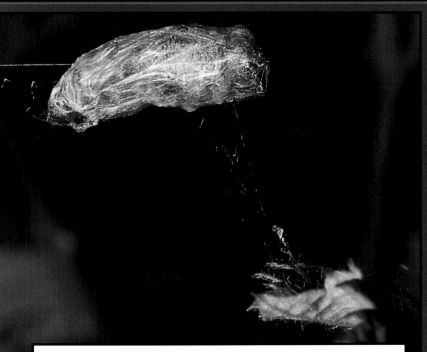

Amazonian spider

WRAP IT UP

For humans, a silk-wrapped package is quite elegant. For spiders, it's dinner. Most spiders, after biting their prey, wrap the poisoned animal in silk threads. An insect bound in silk can be saved for a hungrier day.

BUILDING BRIDGES

A silk bridge makes traveling between bushes and trees a lot easier. Standing in one place, spiders let out a thread for the wind to carry until it snags on another spot. Then the spider draws the strand tight and marches across, laying down more silk to strengthen the bridge.

Spiderlings preparing to balloon away.

THREADS OF STEEL

Silk may look fragile, but it's amazingly sturdy. Some types are three times stronger than a steel thread of the same diameter! Also, for added strength, spiders combine some threads to make thicker strands and may cover threads with a sticky substance. Silk is very flexible, too. Some can be stretched to nearly twice its length without breaking.

A spider web (in background) holds up easily under the strain of water droplets.

AIRBORNE

Silk is a baby spider's ticket to ride. Spiderlings spread out from one another by ballooning. They climb to a high place and point their spinnerets upward. Then they release a strand of silk, which is lifted by a stream of air, and off they go to live on their own, sometimes riding their silk line for 200 feet!

WONDER WEBS

Think of spider webs, and you may imagine a beautiful wheel with delicate spokes. This is the orb web, just one of the many kinds of webs that spiders build. The length of silk that goes into such a construction can be over 60 feet!

A banded garden spider on an orb web.

GOOD VIBES

Orb-web spiders have poor eyesight. But, tuned into vibrations on their web, they can tell the size and location of victims snared in their trap. When the prey is small, the spider dashes to attack. When large, the spider is more careful. If a wasp is caught, some spiders may cut the enemy loose rather than fight.

◀ With every leg on the net, this spider will know when prey has been snared.

▲ AMAZING ORB

Orb webs are the deadliest trap of all for flying insects. Orb-web spiders create this amazing structure of perfectly placed dry and sticky silk in less than an hour—every night! Then they remain head down in the web's center or go to a nearby silk retreat to wait for prey.

NO-NONSENSE NET ▶

Certain spiders can build elastic rectangular webs that fold up. The spider waits, holding the collapsed web like a net in its four *front* legs, hanging close to the ground by its four *back* legs. When insects pass by, the spider drops the net over its victims.

▲ A feast of trapped mayflies is waiting for the spider of this net.

◀ FUNNEL TUNNEL

Funnel weavers trap insects on the ground. They build tornado-shaped webs that are flat and lacy on the top with a funnel in the center. On the bottom, the spider waits. When it feels the vibrations of a passing insect, it races out to make the kill.

▼ HAMMOCK HUNTERS

Some spiders create hammock-shaped silk sheets on bushes or grass. Above, they run crisscrossing lines called scaffolding. Insects trapped in the scaffolding fall onto the hammock where the spider, waiting below, spears them with poison.

▲ WEB CITY

Not all spiders are loners. Social types live in colonies, numbering in the thousands. They create an enormous web that covers a tree, or they link webs to blanket a field. Members recognize each other by walking on the web with special vibrations.

NABBING PREY

All spiders have ways of capturing prey, but each species has its own method. Those spiders that don't wait around for something to fall into a web are more aggressive. And when they strike, they have the tools to fight. They don't have a sticky net that holds prey, but they do have large, powerful jaws with which they grip dinner.

◀ STALKERS

A jumping spider is the most successful active hunter of all the arachnids. It stalks prey the way a cat stalks mice. And when it pounces, it's on target nine times out of ten!

FISH FEEL ▼

Fishing spiders spend their days floating on the leaves of water plants. Dangling their legs over the side, they pick up the vibrations of small fish or insects struggling on the surface. They snatch this prey from the water. They may also "fish," wiggling a leg to look like a worm.

QUICK CATCH▲

Purse-web spiders dig burrows and line them with silk. They extend the silk as a tube, like the finger of a glove, up to the surface of the ground. There, they cover it with dirt and bits of leaves. When prey passes over this trap, the spiders slash the tube and drag the victim inside.

SPIDER EAT SPIDER

Pirate spiders are spider eaters. They're too slow to hunt and can't build webs, but they must kill to eat. Web spiders are their victims. Masters of surprise, pirates sneak onto webs and attack with deadly venom.

◀ In the tropics, huntsman spiders are welcome in people's homes because they eat cockroaches. This one's eating a spider.

SPIT STICK ▼

Imagine a spider that pins its prey with spit! That's the spitting spider. It squirts two gummy streams as far away as two times its body length. While doing so, the spider shakes its jaws from side to side to create a cage of spit that holds the prey captive. Then the spider bites.

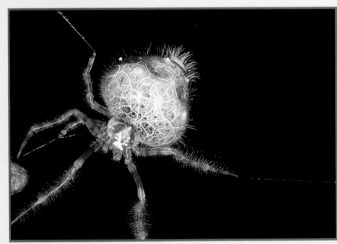

BOLD BOLAS ▲

The prize for capturing prey with the least amount of silk goes to the bolas spider. At twilight, the bolas waits for a moth to appear. Then it drops one short line with a sticky glob on the end. When the moth is struck, it's stuck!

TRAPDOOR

A trapdoor spider digs a burrow and lines it with silk, then builds a door on top. It stays inside, waiting for vibrations from a passing insect. Then it opens the door and attacks.

67

TARANTULA DANCE

BIRD EATER

The most gigantic spiders in the world, with 3-inch bodies and 10-inch leg spans, live in South America. The size of a dinner plate, these tarantulas go after some of the biggest prey. Known as bird-eating spiders, they most often attack nesting birds.

The Colombian purple-bloom birdeater.

Big, hairy spiders are called tarantulas. Their real name, however, is *mygalomorph* (MIG-uh-luh-morf). The true tarantula is the European wolf spider. Its tarantula name comes from the medieval Italian city of Taranto. The people there claimed that the bite of a spider made them dance wildly. The dance was called the tarantella, and the spider became the tarantula.

▼ What does the old carapace of a hairy mygalomorph look like when shed? A collapsed spider.

SENIOR SPIDER

Most spiders live less than a full year. But tarantulas don't even mature to adulthood until they are about 10 or 11 years old. Females may live more than 20 years. The males are not so lucky. They often get eaten by the females right after mating.

UP A TREE

Tarantulas are good at climbing, because, like other wandering spiders, they have pads of hair on their feet. While they're up in trees, they capture frogs, birds, and lizards. With their powerful jaws, they can even crush a small poisonous snake.

This Indian ornamental spider ▶ hangs on tightly to a waxy leaf.

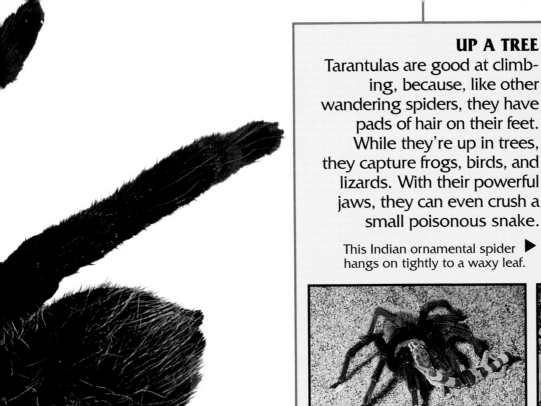

▲ In the desert, fast-moving lizards are a favorite meal.

▲ This striped tarantula emerges from its burrow.

ON DEFENSE ▼

When trouble comes their way, tarantulas make themselves look even more fierce. They raise their front legs, throw themselves back, lift their heads, and expose their fearsome fangs. Now, that's scary!

▲ LOVED TO DEATH

Spiders, like all creatures, suffer when their habitats are destroyed. But the most endangered spider is one that is loved too much. Furry tarantulas, especially the Mexican red-kneed spider, have become so popular as pets, too many have been taken from the wild. Now, sales are being regulated, and some are bred in captivity.

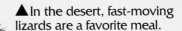

TRICKY SPIDERS

Green lynx spider

Camouflage, or blending into the background, fools both predators and prey. Predators pass by without noticing, and prey gets zapped with a deadly bite. Green lynx spiders know this trick. Their hunting grounds are always green, so they just sit still on green leaves and wait for dinner.

UNDERCOVER ▶

There are spiders that have markings like the lichen, mold, and mosses that grow on trees. Pressed up against a tree, flat as a pancake, these spiders blend in with the bark and cast no shadow.

BEHIND THE BLADE

For the long-jawed orb weaver, posture is a life saver. Clinging to a blade of grass with one pair of legs, it lies head down and extends its other legs until they are straight and narrow. It simply becomes part of the grass until danger goes past.

STILL AS A STICK ▶

This spider from South America chooses to become part of a stick rather than face an attacker.

▲ A goldenrod crab spider nabbing prey.

▲ A crab spider on a woodland sunflower.

The crab spider on these barberry blooms has snagged an unsuspecting fly.

FLOWER POWER

Crab spiders use the power of flowers to snare prey. Color is their weapon. Called flower spiders, they sit on flowers that match their body color. If their body is not just the right tone, they adjust it. Then they wait for a bee, butterfly, or even a fly to buzz by.

▼ This crab spider gives a pink orchid a pretty center, where bees are likely to come looking for pollen.

◀ The crab spider stays just below thistles until dinner arrives, and then, surprise!

71

SPIDERLINGS

There are billions upon billions of spiders on Earth, and more being born every minute. All female spiders lay eggs. Small spiders lay smaller and fewer eggs. Giant bird-eating spiders may lay up to 3,000 eggs, each the size of a pea.

BIG MAMAS ▶

Bigger is better for females in the spider world. The female's body has to hold eggs and produce silk to cover them. And she has to be big enough to protect her young. Some female orb-web spiders weigh as much as 1,000 times more than their mates.

In his courtship dance, the male jumping spider waves his front legs and trots sideways for the female.

◀ SIGN LANGUAGE

When female spiders add scent to their silk, males come running to mate. But a male has to be careful. A big lady spider could mistake a scrawny guy spider for a tasty meal. So, he sends signals. A male web spider may vibrate the silk strands of a female's web in a kind of code. Wandering spiders do a courtship dance.

MOTHER'S WORK ▶

Laying eggs and fertilizing them is the female spider's job. She deposits her eggs on a disc of silk and uses the fluid given to her by the male during mating to fertilize them. Then, like the nursery spider at right, she spins silk around the eggs to make a protective sac.

EGG-CESS BAGGAGE

Certain spiders protect their egg sac with their body. A crab spider (in circle) wraps her legs around her egg sac and stays there until she dies of starvation. The fishing spider (below) carries her sac beneath her body, clasped between her jaws and spinnerets. The sac is so big, the spider tiptoes on all eight legs.

▲ SAC HATCH

Spiderlings break out of their eggs and remain in their egg sac until they are fully developed. If they belong to a species without motherly care, they stay together for a short while. If food is scarce, they may eat a brother or sister before going on their way.

▼ BABY CARRIAGE

Newly hatched wolf spiderlings get a piggyback ride. Their mother cuts open the egg sac for them, and they scramble onto her back. If they fall off, they climb back up the draglines they have attached to her.

▲ NURSERY MOM

It's a dangerous world for spiderlings. But some spider mothers do take care of their young. The nursery-web spider builds a silk tent for her babies and guards them until they all scatter.

BAD BITES

Spiders bite. That's what fangs are for. And they do kill their prey with poison. A bite to humans, however, is almost always harmless, except when it's by the black widow, the brown recluse, or the Sydney funnel-web spider. But deaths from spiders are extremely rare.

The southern black widow has a red hourglass mark on the underside of its lower body.

WIDOW'S WAYS

The female black widow spider has a bad reputation (males do not bite). Actually, she is a shy creature that likes dark places and runs if disturbed. She does live close to people, though. Found in clothes or shoes, she sometimes gets pressed against someone's bare skin. Frightened, she bites!

DYING FOR LOVE

The black widow gets her name from killing her "husband" and making herself a widow. Indeed, she sometimes eats him. But male deaths are not a big loss for the species. The males usually mate only once. And their body, having been eaten, provides nutrients for developing eggs.

The much smaller male carefully approaches his mate.

VICIOUS VENOM

The black widow's venom is one of the deadliest. It's about 15 times more potent than rattlesnake venom, one of the more powerful snake toxins. Lucky for us, we are much larger than the black widow, and the amount of venom in her bite is small. So, several days of discomfort, rather than death, usually follow a bite from a black widow.

COBWEB WEAVER ▼

The black widow is not a very tidy spider. She hangs out around trash piles and dumps, and there she weaves a tangled, woolly mess, called a cobweb. She is one of many cobweb weavers who hang upside-down in the center of the web, waiting for prey to drop in. Then she sucks her victim dry.

◄ DANGER DOWN UNDER

Australia, which suffers from some of the most poisonous snakes in the world, has a spider to match, the Sydney funnel-web spider. Its bite at first causes unbearable pain. Then come convulsions and coma. Fortunately, a cure for the poison has been found.

Western widow

FRIGHTENING FAMILY

As if one were not enough, black widows have relatives. There are northern, western, brown, and red widows.

◄ WRETCHED RECLUSE

The brown recluse has a nasty poisonous bite that grows. It starts out as a small black spot, but the area of dead tissue increases, and six inches of skin can peel away. The victim is left with a wound that is hard to heal and a scar for a souvenir.

Northern widow

75

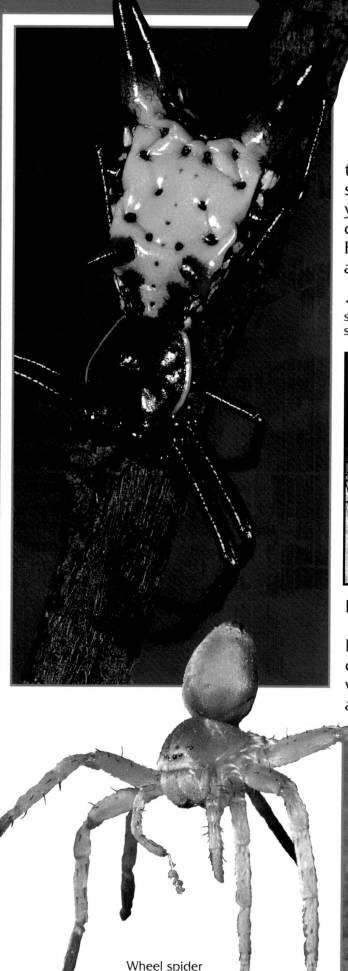

SPECIAL SELECTION

What you picture in your mind when you hear the word "spider" may not be what you actually see. Because there are so many species of spiders, you can be sure that they look very different from one another. Then, too, they don't all act the same. Here, you get a peek at an assortment of artful arthropods.

◀ Don't mistake them for insects! Microthena spiders have hard, spiny lower bodies, which are sometimes very colorful. This arrow-shaped microthena is found in gardens in the eastern United States.

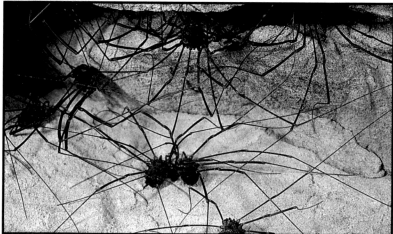

DISAPPEARING ACT ▲

Daddy-long-legs spiders look as frail as feathers, but they get around—especially in cellars and dark corners, where they hang upside-down in loose webs. If alarmed, the daddy-long-legs whirls around, shaking itself and its web so rapidly that they both seem to disappear.

◀ SAND SURFER ▶

The wheel spider of the South African desert travels like a wheel. Tucking in its eight legs to form a circle, the spider rolls away at amazing speeds. Because of the desert's smooth sand and steep dunes, the one-half inch spider can roll at 20 revolutions per second, the same as the wheel of a car traveling 137 miles per hour.

Wheel spider wheeling!

Wheel spider

WATER WORLD

Some spiders live in the water, trapping air bubbles they carry under the surface when they dive. European water spiders live under an air-filled silk tent. There are also about 600 species of sea spiders. They live near the shore or on the bottom of the ocean, where they feed on anemones and other sea creatures.

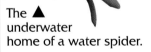

The ▲ underwater home of a water spider.

IN THE DARK ▶

What's a spider without eyes? A cave spider. This one lives in Malaysia.

LONG LEAP

Imagine jumping the length of a football field in a single bound. Jumping spiders make that kind of leap. Only a fifth of an inch long, they can jump 40 times their body length. They do it to eat. Jumping off strong back legs, they can even leap to catch flying insects in midair!

◀ Captured in flight, this jumping spider will probably land on its prey.

77

LIVING WITH SPIDERS

Spiders can look pretty scary, with all those legs and eyes. Some people are really afraid of them. Really afraid. This fear is called arachnophobia (uh-RACK-nuh-foe-bee-uh). A movie by the same name certainly made the most of being afraid of spiders. But spiders aren't that big of a danger to people. They are actually a help.

◀ STUDY A BUDDY

Make your yard a spider home and be an *arachnologist*, a person who studies spiders. Let them build webs on bushes and trees. Don't disturb leaves and stones.

BITE FRIGHT

Getting bitten by a spider can be scary. But if you're healthy, most likely you'll be all right. However, you should go to a doctor. There are antidotes for black widow bites, and sometimes, when the bite is a bad one, painkillers are necessary.

The film that really played on spider terror was *The Incredible Shrinking Man.* Here's a scene where the little guy with a sewing needle takes on a spider.

▼ BUG BUSTER

Spiders eat so many insects, they could make good farmhands. In one experiment in California, wolf spiders consumed enough pests to increase a rice crop. If spiders can be introduced into fields to protect crops, they may be able to help decrease the use of pesticides.

A wolf spider snagging a cicada.

▼ MUFFET'S MEDICINE

Remember Miss Muffet and the spider who sat down beside her? She was a real girl, named Patience, who lived in the 1500s. Her father was a spider expert who made her eat mashed spiders when she was ill. Until the 1800s, many people believed spiders cured illness. They swallowed spiders like pills.

FIRST SPIDER

The name arachnid, for spiders, comes from a Greek legend. Arachne was a girl who outraged the goddess Athena with her beautiful weaving. Arachne became so upset over Athena's anger, she hanged herself. Athena, feeling sorry, turned Arachne into a spider so she could weave forever.

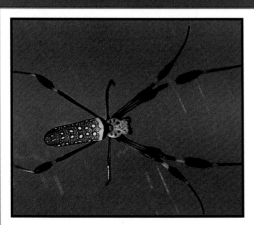

TOOLS OF SILK

People have found many uses for the silk spun by spiders. Silk from the golden silk spider has been used by people in the Caribbean to make fishing nets. Even this black-chinned hummingbird (right) has found that silk can be put to good use.

Golden silk spider

Photo Credits: Lizards

Breck P. Kent: pages 83-84, 86, 95, 97-98
Dwight Kuhn: pages 83-84, 88-89, 97
Zig Leszczynski: pages 82-83, 87-95, 98-102, 104
Dan Nedrelo: page 99
A.B. Sheldon: pages 95, 99-100
Stanley Breeden/DRK: page 91, 102
John Cancalosi/DRK: pages 100, 103
M.C. Chamberlain/DRK: page 91
Michael Fogden/DRK: pages 86-87, 97, 102-103
Joe McDonald/DRK: page 103
David Northcott/DRK: pages 85, 93
T.A. Wiewandt/DRK: page 90
Jeremy Woodhouse/DRK: page 84
Belinda Wright/DRK: page 102
Stephen Dalton/Photo Researchers: page 96
Nathan W. Cohen/Visuals Unlimited: page 105
Gerald & Buff Corsi/Visuals Unlimited: page 96
John Gerlach/Visuals Unlimited: page 91
Thomas Gula/Visuals Unlimited: page 83
Ken Lucas/Visuals Unlimited: pages 85, 104-105
Joe McDonald/Visuals Unlimited: pages 82, 92, 94, 99, 101
Jim Merli/Visuals Unlimited: pages 89, 95-97
David L. Pearson/Visuals Unlimited: page 85
Kjell B. Sandved/Visuals Unlimited: page 101
Tom J. Ulrich/Visuals Unlimited: cover
Dennis Frieborn/Wildlife Collection: page 88
Mauricio Handler/Wildlife Collection: page 90
Martin Harvey/Wildlife Collection: pages 82, 87, 92
Tim Laman/Wildlife Collection: page 83

Scientific Consultant:
David Dickey
American Museum of Natural History

LIZARDS

LOOK! LIZARDS!

Meet the lizards. Some of these four-legged, scaly creatures can lap up an insect and then disappear before you can even blink. Like snakes, turtles, and crocodiles, lizards are reptiles—distant relatives of the dinosaurs.

SUNBATHERS

Have you ever seen a lizard or any other reptile lying in the sun? These creatures are cold-blooded, and need the sun for warmth. In fact, if a lizard becomes too hot or too cold, its body doesn't work properly.

◀ The marine iguana

The sungazer has spiny armor, which it uses for defense.

This Nile monitor lizard has netted a fish.

TOUGH GUY

A lizard's scaly skin is made of keratin, the same material found in your skin, nails, and hair. These tough scales protect the lizard's body from injury.

NO-FAIL TAIL

Most lizards spend their time on land, but some are strong swimmers. Their long, powerful tail helps propel them through the water.

82

LIZARD? NOT! ▶

Salamanders are often mistaken for lizards. They belong to a group of animals called amphibians, which include frogs, toads, and newts. Amphibian skin is soft and moist and without scales. Unlike reptiles, amphibians must lay their eggs in the water.

LIZARD OR SNAKE? ▲

Because its long, legless body resembles that of a snake, the glass lizard is often confused for one. But check its eyes. Like most other lizards, the glass lizard's eyes open and close. Snakes have no eyelids. Their eyes remain open all the time!

◀ ONE OF A KIND

Although lizardlike in appearance, the tuatara is not a lizard. It's the sole survivor of an ancient group of reptiles. Tuataras live on a few scattered islands near New Zealand. They make their home in burrows, which they leave at night to hunt insects.

The Komodo dragon

The dwarf gecko

LIVING ALL OVER

You can find lizards just about anywhere in the world except in cold regions. Many can be found in the tropics. They live in just about every kind of habitat, making their home in trees, water, and underground.

DWARFS TO DRAGONS ▲

Lizards range in size from the one-inch-long dwarf gecko to the ten-foot-long, 365-pound Komodo dragon—and even longer. Some of the smaller lizards fit in your hand, and they're not dangerous to hold. But a Komodo dragon will attack and even kill people!

83

LOTS OF LIZARDS

With more than 3,700 different species, lizards are by far the largest group of reptiles. You may have a picture in your mind of what a lizard is supposed to look like. But lizards look very different from one another. Just compare iguanas, monitors, chameleons, agamids, geckos, skinks, and some other, common lizards.

◄ SUPER GRIP
Most all lizards have five, clawed toes, and can scuttle up some kind of surface. Geckos probably have the most incredible grip, because they have brushlike hooks on their feet. They are often seen at night in houses in tropical regions, running across the ceilings or climbing the glass in windows! But geckos do even more. The most vocal lizards, they make a noise that sounds like…"geck-oh, geck-oh."

ALL-AMERICAN ►
This lizard, known as an anole, is found only in the southern United States. It's known as the American "chameleon" because it can change its color—from green to brown—and blend in with the background. But the anole is actually a small iguana.

MIGHTY MONITOR ▲
Among lizards, the monitors are the mightiest. There are about 30 different kinds, including the fierce Komodo dragon. Not all are huge, but the big ones are really big. The Nile monitor, which is medium-sized, grows up to seven feet.

84

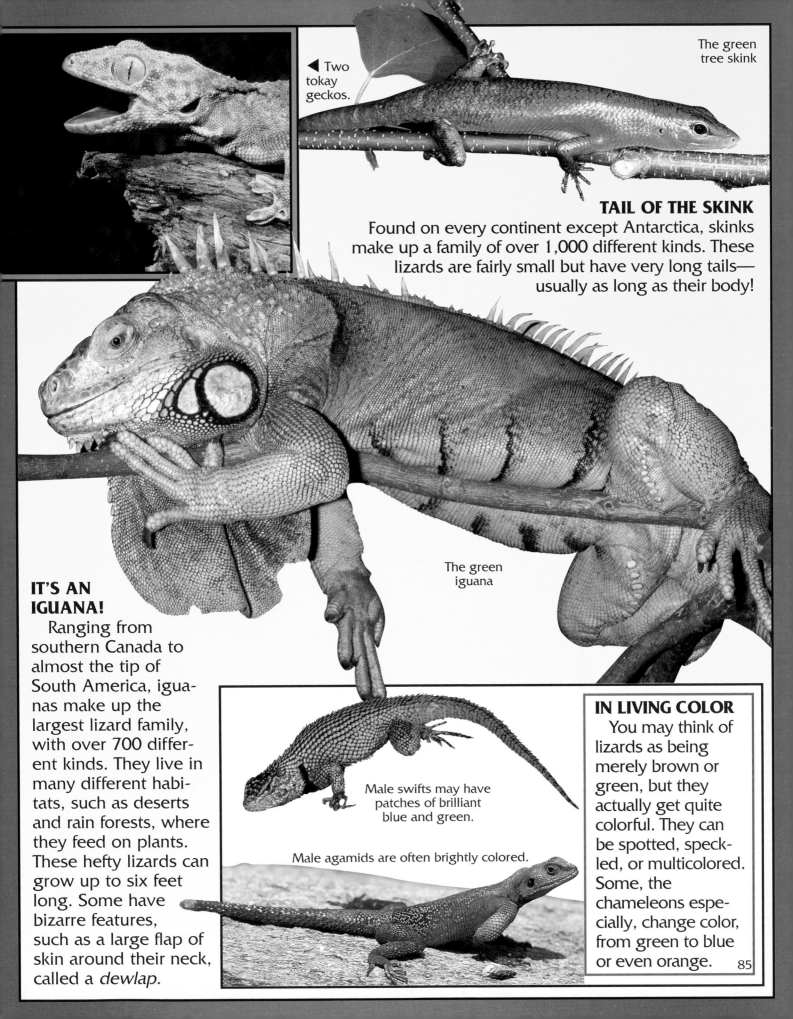

◄ Two tokay geckos.

The green tree skink

TAIL OF THE SKINK

Found on every continent except Antarctica, skinks make up a family of over 1,000 different kinds. These lizards are fairly small but have very long tails— usually as long as their body!

The green iguana

IT'S AN IGUANA!

Ranging from southern Canada to almost the tip of South America, iguanas make up the largest lizard family, with over 700 different kinds. They live in many different habitats, such as deserts and rain forests, where they feed on plants. These hefty lizards can grow up to six feet long. Some have bizarre features, such as a large flap of skin around their neck, called a *dewlap.*

Male swifts may have patches of brilliant blue and green.

Male agamids are often brightly colored.

IN LIVING COLOR

You may think of lizards as being merely brown or green, but they actually get quite colorful. They can be spotted, speckled, or multicolored. Some, the chameleons especially, change color, from green to blue or even orange. 85

BODY HEAT

The web-footed gecko basks in the early morning sun. Only when its body has soaked up enough heat will it start hunting.

All reptiles are unable to produce their own body heat the way mammals and birds can. They need the sun's heat to warm their body. Because of their dependence on the sun, most lizards are found in places with warm climates. Many make their home in the desert.

Usually known for their bright colors, chameleons are a different story in the desert. Here, camouflage means blending in with sand and rock.

In the desert, the collared lizard hops from rock top to rock top in search of insects and smaller lizards to feed on.

NO SWEAT

Lizards don't sweat, or lose water through their thick, scaly skin. This ability allows them to live in dry desert climates. But there's a limit to how much heat they can stand. Desert temperatures sometimes reach 120°F. If a desert iguana's temperature rises above 110°F, it could die. To escape this danger, it has to find shade.

A desert iguana

This sand-diving lizard is checking the temperature.

DESERT DIG ▲

To escape the scorching midday sun, some lizards burrow below the surface of the sun-baked sand where the temperatures are cooler.

▼ BURROWING GIANTS

Found only on a few small Indonesian islands, the Komodo dragon uses its ten, long, sharp claws to hollow out a burrow in the side of a small hill. Here is where it escapes the hot midday sun, and where it snuggles for warmth when the sun goes down.

DANCING FEET ▲

When the sand becomes too hot to walk on, a shovel-snouted lizard begins a strange dance to find relief. First it lifts its two left feet off the burning sand, then its two right feet. For the final step, it lifts all four feet while it rests on its belly.

87

WHAT'S FOR DINNER?

Most lizards are meat eaters, dining on insects and other prey. Their small, sharp teeth grab and hold their catch while their jaws make a series of quick, snapping movements over the animal. Then they swallow the prey whole.

Having ▶ snared a rodent, this tegu is swallowing its prey.

▲ GREAT SHOT

In less than one second, the chameleon can catch dinner. Its tongue is an amazing hunting weapon. Stretching the combined length of the chameleon's body and tail, the tongue has at its end a sticky pad that picks up insects. Once dinner is attached, the tongue will recoil back inside the mouth.

CACTUS EATERS

Some lizards, such as iguanas and agamids, are vegetarians, preferring to eat plants rather than animals for dinner. It may seem astounding, but iguanas can bite into and eat cactus without so much as an "ouch."

NIGHT HUNTERS

All geckos are meat eaters, and most are active at night. They feed mainly on insects and spiders, but the larger geckos can overpower other lizards, birds, and even small mammals. The geckos that make good night hunters have huge eyes like a cat's. The vertical pupils open wide at night to let in as much light as possible.

EGG EATERS ▶

The venomous Gila (HE-luh) monster is one of only two poisonous lizards in the world. Found in the south-western United States, the Gila monster crawls too slowly to chase down its dinner. Instead, it feeds on eggs and newborn animals.

HEARTY APPETITE

The Komodo dragon is so big that it eats goats, pigs, and deer. With sharp teeth like a shark's, a dragon can finish off a sixty-pound dinner in about fifteen minutes.

▼ TASTING AIR

Some lizards, like the monitors, taste the air with a forked tongue, much like snakes do. In this way, lizards can track down prey and avoid predators.

GETTING AROUND

Lizards depend on quickness to hunt and keep safe. Most have four legs and use them to move at high speeds. Nature has also given these creatures extra equipment, custom-designed for the places in which they live.

DEEP-SEA DIVER

The marine iguana of the Galapagos Islands is the only lizard truly at home in saltwater. A vegetarian with little to choose from on the island, the iguana dives as deep as thirty feet to find seaweed and algae. While diving for food, the marine iguana can stop its heart completely for three minutes in order to save oxygen.

FLYING DRAGON ▶

When the agamid known as the flying dragon spots a green vine snake slithering closer and closer, it moves into action. It raises up and expands the loose flaps of skin along its body in an attempt to look larger and more ferocious. Right before the snake strikes, this tricky lizard glides safely to a nearby tree.

WORMY LIZARD ▼

Not all lizards have four legs, especially not the ones that live underground. Some have only two legs or no legs at all. Without legs, it's easier to slither through the earth, tunneling in search of insects and worms

This two-legged worm lizard lives in the Sonoran Desert in Baja, Mexico.

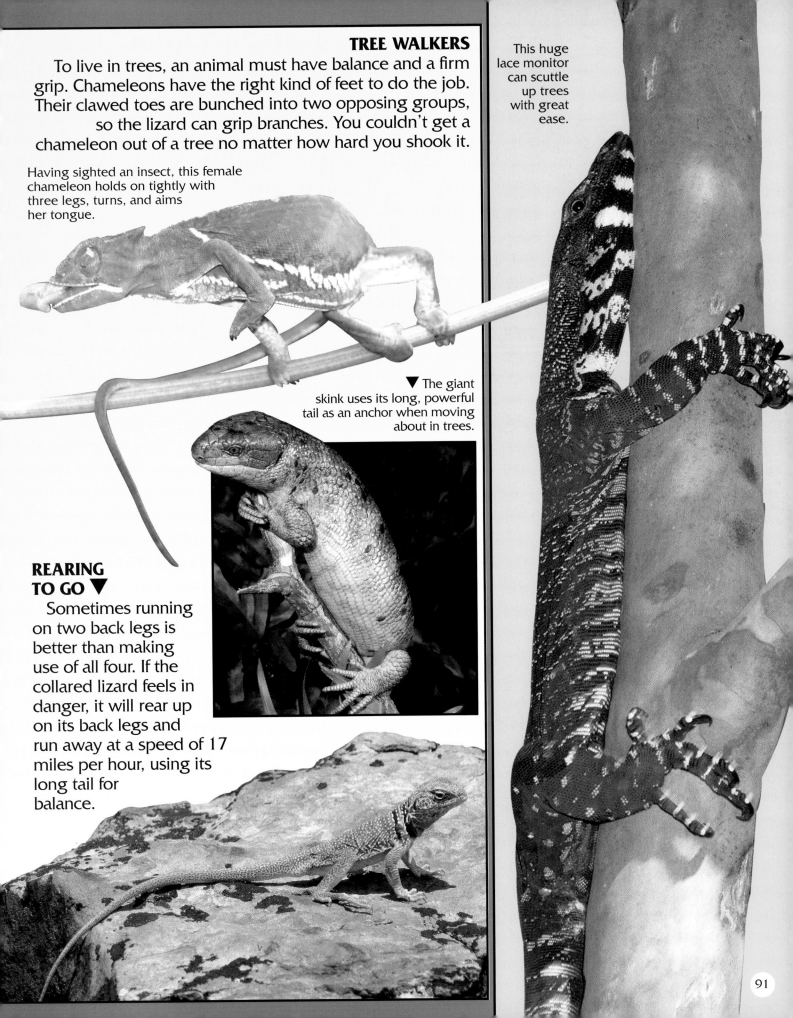

TREE WALKERS

To live in trees, an animal must have balance and a firm grip. Chameleons have the right kind of feet to do the job. Their clawed toes are bunched into two opposing groups, so the lizard can grip branches. You couldn't get a chameleon out of a tree no matter how hard you shook it.

Having sighted an insect, this female chameleon holds on tightly with three legs, turns, and aims her tongue.

This huge lace monitor can scuttle up trees with great ease.

▼ The giant skink uses its long, powerful tail as an anchor when moving about in trees.

REARING TO GO ▼

Sometimes running on two back legs is better than making use of all four. If the collared lizard feels in danger, it will rear up on its back legs and run away at a speed of 17 miles per hour, using its long tail for balance.

91

KINGS OF COLOR

If you want to see spectacular lizards, look at chameleons. There are about 85 different kinds, and they all have amazing equipment. They have a tongue as long as their body, eyes that can look in two different directions at one time, and a specialized tail and clawed feet that keep them secure in the branches. But chameleons are probably best known for their amazing color changes.

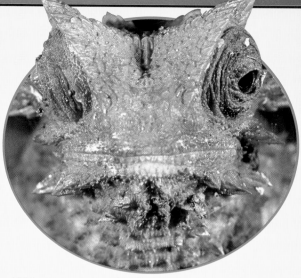

With one eye looking forward and one eye pointed back, this dwarf chameleon looks out for prey and predators.

▲ Here, the carpet chameleon boasts both spots and stripes.

MAGIC PIGMENT

What gives chameleons their color? Tiny particles of material known as pigment, located in the chameleon's skin. Chameleons can be brown, yellow, green, gray, red, or even striped or spotted. It all depends on how and where the pigment moves.

◀ This veiled chameleon is equipped with a helmet-shaped head, sharp claws, and remarkable stripes.

TRUE OR FALSE?

Does a chameleon camouflage itself? No. A chameleon does not "choose" to blend in with its environment. It does not "decide" to change its color. The change happens automatically because of the animal's temperature, the amount of light it's exposed to, or its mood. For example, as a chameleon becomes cooler, it will begin to darken in order to absorb more sunlight.

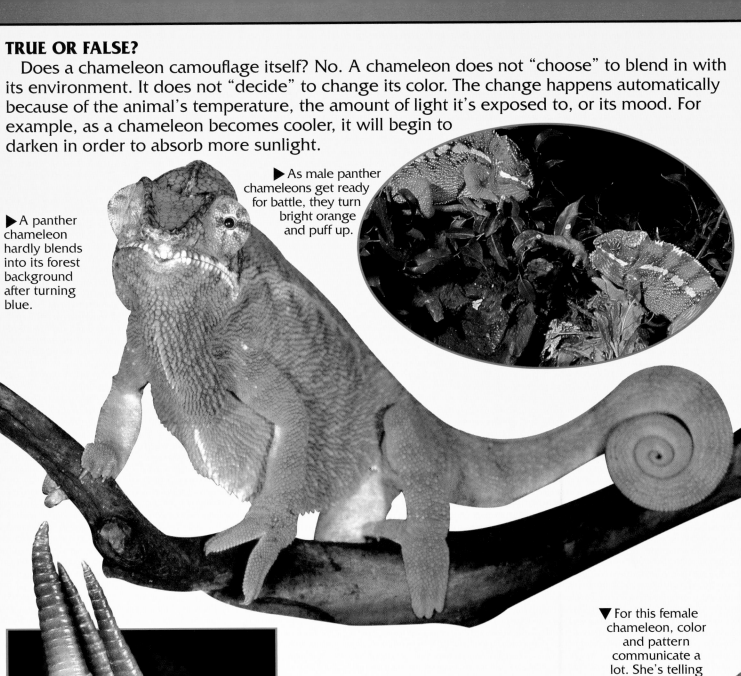

▶ A panther chameleon hardly blends into its forest background after turning blue.

▶ As male panther chameleons get ready for battle, they turn bright orange and puff up.

▼ For this female chameleon, color and pattern communicate a lot. She's telling everyone she's going to have babies.

DECKED OUT ▲

Chameleons are really decorated! They have ornaments such as crests on their back or tail, and flaps and spikes hanging down from their chin. The male Jackson chameleon, shown above, has three horns and a small crested helmet.

BABY BOOM

From courtship to birth, baby-making varies from one kind of lizard to another. Usually when courting, males become more brightly colored. But some also do special "dances" to get a female's attention. Most females lay eggs and leave their unhatched babies behind. But some carry the eggs inside their body until they're ready to hatch.

LITTLE IGUANAS

Most mother lizards lay eggs with tough, leathery shells. The green iguana may lay up to 40 at one time. The baby lizards that emerge from the eggs are miniature versions of their parents. Right after they hatch, the babies can find their own food.

WRESTLE MANIA

At the start of each mating season, male Bengal monitor lizards try to impress the ladies with their strength. They wrestle each other for the privilege of mating with a female. It may look like a dance, but it's serious business!

When the ▶ male African rainbow agama wants to get a female's attention, he completes a series of push-ups.

CHISELING OUT

All baby lizards that hatch from eggs have a pointed *egg tooth* on their snout. They use the tooth to chisel their way out of the eggshell.

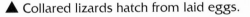
▲ Collared lizards hatch from laid eggs.

▲ THANKS, MOM

The five-lined skink mother doesn't leave her babies to fend for themselves. She coils herself around her eggs and guards them against egg-eating predators.

BIRTHDAY

In cooler climates, eggs buried in the ground would not stay warm enough to hatch. In these places, lizards incubate the eggs inside their body, where it is warm. Some lizards, such as the Jackson chameleon, give birth to fully developed babies.

This baby Jackson ▲ chameleon shows off for dad.

▼ Bearded dragon babies

SAFETY IN NUMBERS

Lizard babies may start fighting each other very early on, trying to establish a territory. But some babies stick together until they're old enough to take care of themselves. For the first twelve months of life, emerald lizards stay together. When attacked, they scatter in all directions, confusing their attacker and giving themselves a few seconds to escape.

THAT'S AMAZING!

Have you ever seen a lizard with a beard? Do you know there's one lizard that can walk on water? Lizards are amazing. Their antics and armor really set them apart!

◀ WALKING ON WATER

The basilisk lizard has an incredible method of escape from its enemies. It rears up on its hind legs and runs across the surface of water. Moving quickly on long, wide toes, the basilisk can take several strides before its body breaks the water's surface and sinks in.

BIG BEARD ▶

This lizard does have a beard—a chin full of spiky armor! Known as the bearded dragon, it uses its armor to frighten enemies. It inflates its body, opens its mouth, and expands its big, spiny throat. That's a frightening sight and a big signal to stand clear!

SALT SHAKERS

Marine iguanas are really resourceful when it comes to finding food. They swim the sea looking for seaweed. There's one problem, though. They swallow a large amount of water and get a huge overdose of salt. But their body has developed an amazing trick. It shakes out the salt through special glands in the nasal cavities.

NO-FAIL TAIL

The chameleon is one lizard that can hang by its tail from a branch like a monkey. All lizards have fantastic tails. Some tails are long and are used for balance. Some can be discarded to distract enemies so that the lizard can escape. But only a few are built for strength and allow the lizard to hang out in trees.

THIRST QUENCHER

Getting a drink of water in the desert is not that easy, unless you're a thorny devil. This lizard has sharp spikes covering its body for protection. But the spikes also provide drinking water. Overnight, dew condenses on the thorns, and the water trickles along tiny grooves in the skin to the thorny devil's mouth.

WINDSHIELD WIPER

Most lizards have eyelids, which protect the eyes and help keep them clean. Geckos, however, do not. Instead, they use their long tongue like a windshield wiper, rolling it over their eyes to keep their vision clear!

97

BYE-BYE SKIN

Lizards never stop growing! Because their skin does not grow with them, they have to shed it. A few use shedding as a defense. Geckos are covered with a very loose layer of skin. The slightest amount of pressure from an attack causes the skin to come off. The lizard escapes, and the attacker is left with an old suit.

RUN OR HIDE

Lizards are survivors. One of the reasons they are so successful is that they've developed very effective ways to defend themselves. Most lizards are small creatures who depend on speed and quickness rather than brute strength. Their first line of defense, in fact, is to run or hide.

TIGHT SQUEEZE ▼

While basking in the sun, lizards like to stay close to a rocky crevice or burrow where they can retreat if threatened. But the chuckwalla lizard has an additional defense. When it gets between two rocks, it takes several deep breaths and inflates its body with air. Wedged in tightly, the chuckwalla becomes impossible for an attacker to even budge.

IN THE HOLE ▼

Hiding can be very simple in the desert. A lizard can simply burrow beneath the sand. With only its face showing, this sandy-colored horned lizard could easily be overlooked by a predator.

GOOD PLANNING ▲

A basilisk lizard knows how to take a nap. Living in Brazil's tropical rain forest, it crawls out to the tip of a thin branch that extends out over a small stream. When a hungry snake slithers too close, the branch shakes. With this warning, the basilisk drops into the water, safely out of the snake's reach.

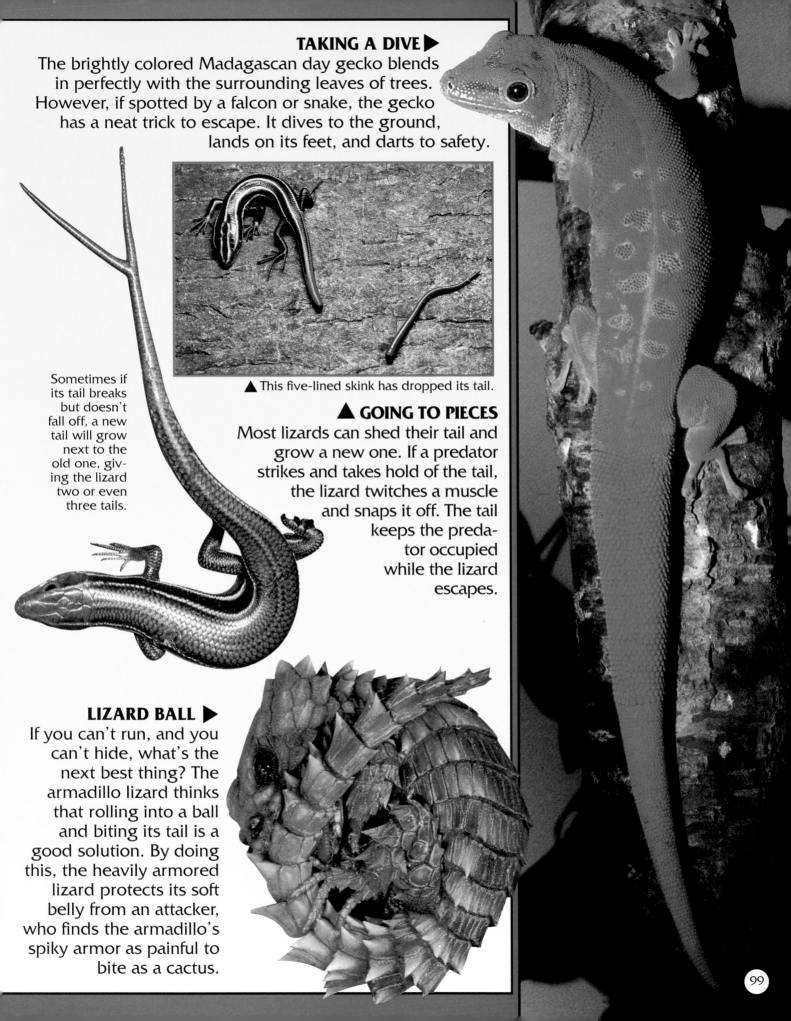

TAKING A DIVE ▶

The brightly colored Madagascan day gecko blends in perfectly with the surrounding leaves of trees. However, if spotted by a falcon or snake, the gecko has a neat trick to escape. It dives to the ground, lands on its feet, and darts to safety.

▲ This five-lined skink has dropped its tail.

Sometimes if its tail breaks but doesn't fall off, a new tail will grow next to the old one, giving the lizard two or even three tails.

▲ GOING TO PIECES

Most lizards can shed their tail and grow a new one. If a predator strikes and takes hold of the tail, the lizard twitches a muscle and snaps it off. The tail keeps the predator occupied while the lizard escapes.

LIZARD BALL ▶

If you can't run, and you can't hide, what's the next best thing? The armadillo lizard thinks that rolling into a ball and biting its tail is a good solution. By doing this, the heavily armored lizard protects its soft belly from an attacker, who finds the armadillo's spiky armor as painful to bite as a cactus.

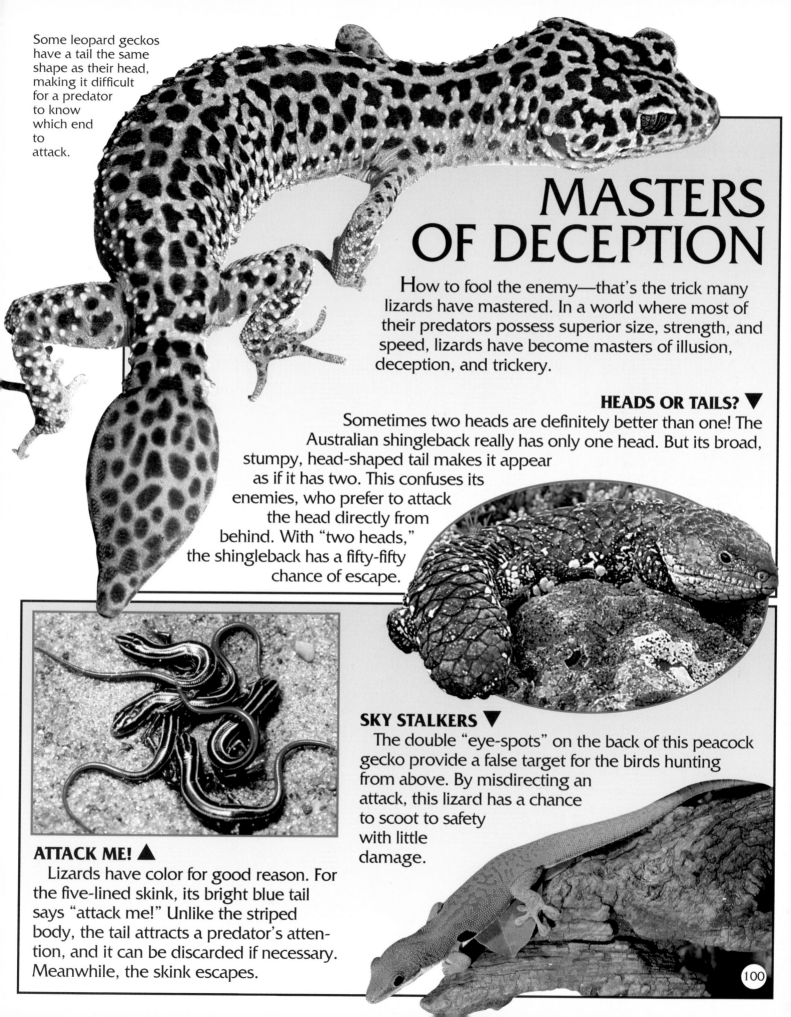

Some leopard geckos have a tail the same shape as their head, making it difficult for a predator to know which end to attack.

MASTERS OF DECEPTION

How to fool the enemy—that's the trick many lizards have mastered. In a world where most of their predators possess superior size, strength, and speed, lizards have become masters of illusion, deception, and trickery.

HEADS OR TAILS? ▼

Sometimes two heads are definitely better than one! The Australian shingleback really has only one head. But its broad, stumpy, head-shaped tail makes it appear as if it has two. This confuses its enemies, who prefer to attack the head directly from behind. With "two heads," the shingleback has a fifty-fifty chance of escape.

ATTACK ME! ▲

Lizards have color for good reason. For the five-lined skink, its bright blue tail says "attack me!" Unlike the striped body, the tail attracts a predator's attention, and it can be discarded if necessary. Meanwhile, the skink escapes.

SKY STALKERS ▼

The double "eye-spots" on the back of this peacock gecko provide a false target for the birds hunting from above. By misdirecting an attack, this lizard has a chance to scoot to safety with little damage.

WHERE'S THAT LIZARD?

Camouflage is a nifty little trick. Many lizards are naturally colored to blend in with their habitat, whether it's in the trees of a rain forest, in the desert sand, or on a forest floor.

▲ If you were walking by this tree, would you see this leaf-tailed gecko?

▲ Can you spot a gliding gecko in this photo?

A panther chameleon

FREEZE!

True masters of deception, chameleons know that, when you want to escape a predator, it's sometimes better just to stand still. In the face of danger, chameleons stop and remain motionless. Their color usually blends with their environment, making them doubly hard to spot. An attacker will often go right on by.

PLAYING POSSUM

Some chameleons "play possum," or pretend to be dead. When cornered, the chameleon suddenly drops to the ground on its side, stretches its feet out stiffly, and remains motionless. Most predators prefer a fresh kill to a dead meal, so they sometimes walk away. If not, they at least relax their guard long enough so that the chameleon can run to safety.

101

◀ Standing up on its hind legs, this monitor lizard takes on a threatening posture.

SCARY MOVES

When escape is blocked and a hungry predator is closing in, nature has provided lizards with one last line of defense. A lizard will turn aggressive, trying to scare or intimidate its would-be killer into backing down. If that fails, watch out! The lizard will attack.

▼ STAY AWAY!

If cornered, the Australian frilled lizard rears up on its hind legs, opens its mouth wide, and unfolds the enormous frill around its head. If its attacker is still around, the lizard swings its head to and fro, lashes its long, whiplike tail back and forth, and sounds a long, angry hissss!

POP EYES

A frightened helmeted lizard tries to make himself look as large and ferocious as possible. It raises the bony "helmet" on the back of its skull, inflates the flap of skin around its neck, and bugs out its eyes. After seeing this huge frightening head, many predators realize that they weren't quite as hungry as they thought.

◀ This anole tries to frighten off an intruder by inflating a brightly colored dewlap.

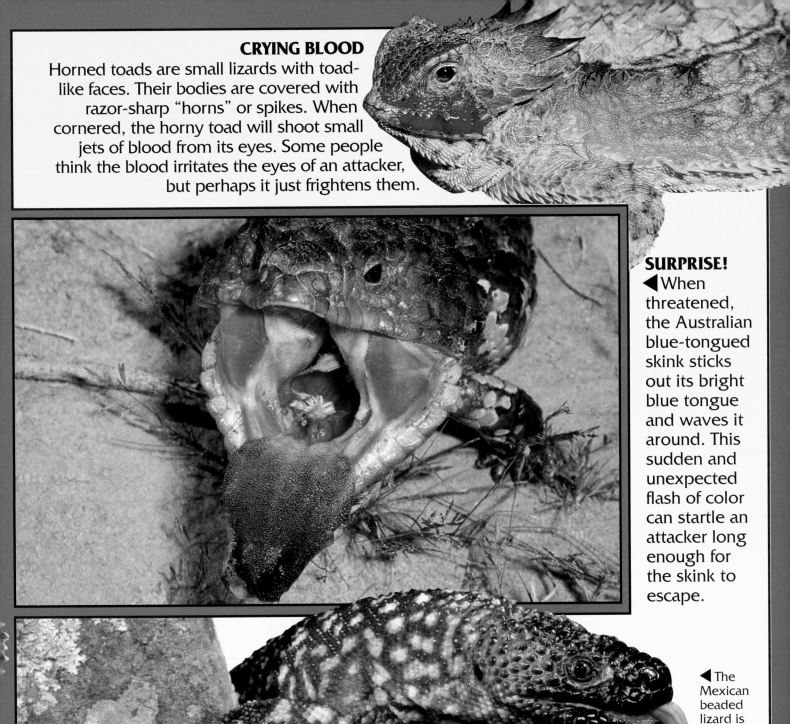

CRYING BLOOD

Horned toads are small lizards with toad-like faces. Their bodies are covered with razor-sharp "horns" or spikes. When cornered, the horny toad will shoot small jets of blood from its eyes. Some people think the blood irritates the eyes of an attacker, but perhaps it just frightens them.

SURPRISE!

◄When threatened, the Australian blue-tongued skink sticks out its bright blue tongue and waves it around. This sudden and unexpected flash of color can startle an attacker long enough for the skink to escape.

◄The Mexican beaded lizard is one of only two poisonous lizards.

SLOW DEATH

The Mexican beaded lizard and Gila (Hee-la) monster are poisonous. Once they bite their enemy, they clamp onto it with their teeth. As the lizard struggles to keep its grip, the poison slowly trickles into the wound. The lizard's venom can kill a small animal but rarely kills people.

A LOOK AHEAD

Today a great many lizards are in danger of being killed, due mainly to loss of habitat and hunting. People can help prevent their endangerment. By not purchasing products made from lizards, they can give hunters fewer reasons to kill these incredible creatures.

Dumeril's monitor

Pacific monitor

A TASTY TREAT ▼

Believe it or not, some people find lizards to be tasty treats. In South and Central America, iguanas are a delicacy often served to visiting relatives and important guests. However, this custom is not a huge threat to the lizard population.

THE PRICE OF BEAUTY ▲

Monitor lizards are beautiful, but they pay a price. Although it is illegal to hunt them, monitors are killed for their skin, which is used to make lizard-skin boots and shoes, pocketbooks, belts, wallets, and briefcases.

POPULAR PETS

For some people, having an exotic pet like a lizard is fashionable. But many lizards die while being captured or transported to pet shops. Of those that survive, a great many die because they are unhappy and unaccustomed to living in captivity.

◀ **DEADLY COMPETITION**

For years, the Galapagos Island iguana was hunted for sport. Today, something else threatens its existence. Goats, brought onto the island by farmers and ranchers, compete with the iguana for available but scarce plant life.

DRAGON SLAYERS ▼

Farmers shoot Komodo dragons to protect livestock, but they are not the only dragon slayers. To many people, the Komodo dragon is a frightening creature. Out of this fear and a lack of knowledge, many Komodos have been killed. There are fewer than 1,000 Komodo dragons left. Their endangerment has prompted the Indonesian government to make it illegal to kill them. Now these well known dragons are a treasured tourist attraction.

▲ **HABITAT DESTRUCTION**

Because the trees in which it lives are being razed, and the land is being cleared for homes, the long-tailed Fijian banded iguana is in serious trouble. Having lost much of its habitat, there is nowhere to hide newly laid eggs, which become easy pickings for the banded iguana's enemy, the mongoose.

Index

Glossary

Albino: Animal that has a decreased amount of pigment, or color, in its skin, hair, and eyes.

Arachnologist: Person who studies spiders and their relatives.

Arachnophobia: Fear of spiders and their relatives.

Arthropod: Animal with legs and joints but no backbone; arthropods include shrimp, crabs, and spiders.

Camouflage: Way that an animal disguises and protects itself by appearing to blend into its surroundings.

Carapace: Tough suit of armor that protects the soft body parts on animals that have skeletons on the outside of their bodies.

Carnivore: Animal that eats the flesh of other animals.

Cold-blooded: Having a body temperature that is not regulated internally but adapts to the temperature of surrounding air or water; reptiles and amphibians are cold-blooded.

Constrictor: Snake, such as a python or boa, that squeezes its prey until it can no longer breathe.

Death-feigning: Method by which an animal pretends that it is dead to protect itself from predators.

Dewlap: Flap of skin around a lizard's neck.

Diurnal: Animal that is active during the day.

Dorsal Scales: Skin on a snake's back.

Dragline: Double thread trailing from behind a spider; helps the spider to escape in times of danger.

Echolocation: Process in which creatures navigate and find food using their ears; by making noises that bounce off objects, bats and other animals can determine if an object or prey is nearby.

Egg Tooth: Pointed tooth that baby lizards use to chisel their way out of their eggshells.

Endangered: Animal that is threatened with extinction.

Exoskeleton: Hard, outer covering of insects, lobsters, and crabs that protects organs inside.

Food Chain: Series of living things in which each feeds upon the one below it and in turn is eaten by the one above it; cycle repeats itself until the tiniest animal eats the bacteria that is left behind from the largest animal.

Habitat: Natural surroundings of a particular animal.

Herbivore: Animal that eats only fruits, plants, and vegetables.

Herpetologist: Scientist who studies snakes and other reptiles and amphibians.

Hibernate: To rest, sleep, and remain inactive through the winter; animals that hibernate survive on the food stored in their bodies until spring.

Melanistic: Having an increased amount of black pigment, or color.

Mimicry: Method by which an animal protects itself from predators by resembling its surroundings or another animal; a non-poisonous animal that acts like a dangerous animal is mimicking.

Molt: To shed skin, hair, or hard outside covering; when a spider grows, it replaces the armor that protects its soft body parts with a bigger one.

Nocturnal: Animal that is active at night.

Pedipalps: Leglike features on the side of a spider's mouth used to hold prey.

Pigment: Natural substance that gives color in skin, eyes, and hair.

Predator: Animal that hunts other animals for food.

Preserve: Large tract of land, set aside by law, for animals to live on.

Prey: An animal that is hunted by other animals for food.

Regeneration: Re-growth of a damaged part of an animal's body.

Roost: To rest, or perch; also, the place where an animal sleeps, hibernates, and has babies.

Spectacle: Scale covering a snake's eyes.

Spinnerets: Flexible, fingerlike tubes by which spiders and other insects spin threads for webs or cocoons.

Ultrasound: High-pitched noises that humans cannot hear.

Venom: Poisonous liquid secreted by some animals.

Ventral Scales: Skin on a snake's belly that helps it move and slither.

Warm-blooded: Having a high body temperature that is regulated internally and is not affected by surroundings; birds and mammals are warm-blooded.